FORGOTTEN
ENGLISH

FORGOTTEN
ENGLISH

Jeffrey Kacirk

WILLIAM MORROW AND COMPANY, INC.
New York

It is the policy of William Morrow and Company, Inc., and its imprints and
affiliates, recognizing the importance of preserving what has been written, to print
the books we publish on acid-free paper, and we exert our best efforts to that end.

Library of Congress Cataloging-in-Publication Data

Kacirk, Jeffrey.
Forgotten English / Jeffrey Kacirk.—1st ed.
p.   cm.
Includes bibliographical references and index.
ISBN 0-688-15018-7 (acid-free paper)
1. English language—Obsolete words—Glossaries, vocabularies, etc.
I. Title.
PE1667.K33   1997

CIP
422—dc21
97-15228

Printed in the United States of America

First Edition

9   10

BOOK DESIGN BY LEAH S. CARLSON

Acknowledgments

I wish to thank my wife, Karen, for her help as a sounding board, in proofreading, and most of all, for her ability to provide me with balance throughout this project. I would also like to acknowledge my father for passing along his love of the unique.

My heartfelt appreciation goes to the British Library and London's Guildhall Library for graciously allowing me access to their extensive collections of historical publications, and to Oxford University and its Press for excellence in compiling an unparalleled treasury of the English language.

I would like to recognize the authors of my source materials, for without their contributions from long ago, my work would not have been possible. Like the special old words they contain, most of the beautiful and fascinating works found in the bibliography have disappeared only because succeeding generations have produced such a profusion of descendants. But, like the stars, which are only visible on a clear night, their endurance helps us to recall our origins.

Contents

CONTENTS

Introduction

The English language, like any other living thing, is continually in a state of flux. Just as cells in our bodies die each day and are replaced with new ones, an almost imperceptible attrition in vocabulary regularly takes place, balancing the hundreds of fledgling terms that make their way into our conversations and dictionaries each year. Nineteenth-century lexicographer Charles Mackay shared this view of the English language as a metaphysical organism with a voracious appetite:

> *It borrows, it steals, it assimilates what words it pleases from all points of the compass, and asks no questions of them but that they shall express thoughts and describe more accurately than any of the old words beside which they are invited to take their places.*

Change is true of all languages, which grow and decline as a result of societal needs and artistic creation, but is particularly prevalent in English, the most dynamic of tongues.

In fact, the richness and maturity of a language may be gauged by the volume and quality of words it can afford to lose. In this regard, English has had no equal in the sheer volume of expressions it has shed over the centuries. These lost words, memorials of a language's earlier stages, form the basis of *Forgotten English*.

Language is among the most durable links we have with the people of earlier times, despite the fact that words continue to disappear for any number of reasons. Not uncommonly, some have been swept aside by substitutes that look and sound more elegant. An exchange of this nature allowed "adulterer" to supplant the more homespun *gandermooner*, which took into account what ganders were known to do while their mates hatched a nestful of eggs. Verbal grace also undoubtedly precipitated the succession of "witness" over *testificator*, and influenced the fall of the colorful but clumsy term *clapperclaw*, which was outlasted by the simpler verb "to scold." Some expressions faded even without replacements as societal values, interests, and tastes changed. Long ago, *cuillage* described a Scottish custom that allowed a lord the right of first refusal with his vassal's bride on their wedding night. Today, a demand by the owner of a company to exercise a similar right would be met with outrage, ridicule, laughter, or perhaps a lawsuit for sexual harassment.

Many terms have perished as a direct result of technological changes. The *bread rasp*, a tool once used by any baker worth his salt, disappeared as more reliable ovens and baking conditions eliminated the need to file off burnt portions of bread crust. Likewise, we no longer have occasion to speak of a *swelk*, the sound produced when butter separated from milk in a revolving churn, a device most people have never heard of or even seen. Seldom does the need arise to differentiate between how clean a water-washed floor is compared to its cleanliness after merely being swept, once known as *besom-clean.*

Scientific investigation has taken its toll on words via the erosion of old customs and myths. The Scottish *quhaip*, an evil spirit that was thought to carry off evil-doers at night with its long curved bill, is long gone. When looking deeply into someone's eyes, once called "looking [for] babies in the eyes," we no longer search for the image of an arrow-shooting infant reflected by the pupils, believed in Shakespeare's day to be Cupid in miniature. Folklore depends heavily on language, as without adequate expressions, culturally developed explanations and beliefs would be difficult to transmit. And, in requiring special words, folklore molds and enriches language.

Not until the nineteenth century did a movement of linguists, lexicographers, and glossarists, including Charles Mackay, Robert Nares, John Jamieson, James Halliwell, and Walter Skeat, perceive a need to track down and catalog an ever-growing number of dead and dying archaic and dialectic relics whose offspring were often used unknowingly in conversation. This group was among the first to realize that, as in the Welsh language, individual words were fast disappearing in the wake of standardized English. These pioneers differed from their predecessors—the most famous of whom was Samuel Johnson—whose main interests were the presentation and homogenization of "usable" English, particularly its spelling.

A goal in creating this work was to better acquaint the reader with a few of the more interesting and forgotten expressions, which can lead to a better understanding of the people who applied these gems, and the times they reflect. The English language becomes more multidimensional when curious old words are recognized as noteworthy aspects of bygone eras. My intent, like that of some of the giants of word-gathering whose work I accessed and perhaps will help to preserve, was to allow these fascinating old words to echo across time and influence new readers as they have me.

Folk remedies and recipes are presented primarily for their historic interest, and not necessarily for their medical or culinary potential. Some are, in fact, nothing short of toxic, or at least nauseating. They should not be misconstrued as representing health care advice of any kind, though some may resemble modern treatments offered by herbalists and other health care professionals.

Entries were selected on the basis of their colorful historical associations, etymologies, unique sound, variety, unusual meanings, or changes in their meanings over time. Quotations have been altered only when necessary for the reader's convenience, understanding, and enjoyment, to clarify archaic punctuation, or to add a few explanatory words, indicated by brackets. Some quotations have been abridged, but only when the omissions were lengthy, divergent in subject matter, or superfluous to the text. Every attempt has been made to preserve the integrity of the original texts while bearing in mind that, as Shakespeare said, "Brevity is [still] the soul of wit."

Chronology

U nderstandably, scholars' opinions vary regarding exact time periods in the evolution of English and its dialects. Dates are useful for organizational purposes, but do not allow for the inevitable overlap found in most historical studies. For convenience, "Anglo-Saxon" and "Old English" shall refer to the period from about 450, when German tribes began to arrive and settle in the British Isles, until the 1100s.

"Middle English" could be said to have flourished between the 1100s and late fifteenth century, prompted by the English defeat at the hands of the French at Hastings in 1066, a watershed date for German-based Old English. The Middle English period, marked by a strong French linguistic influence, bridged Old English and semimodern English, and included part of the Renaissance, which lasted from the late fourteenth to the sixteenth centuries. (The expressions "popery" and "popish" refer to English Christianity before the pope's ouster from Britain in 1536–1540.)

The forty-five-year Elizabethan period, lasting from 1558–1603, roughly concluded the English Renaissance, although Shakespeare's death thirteen years later perhaps serves as a better milestone for English language style. England's Victorian era, characterized by increased congealment and standardization of English, showed signs of developing more than a decade before Victoria's coronation in 1837, and persisted by momentum well beyond her death in 1901.

Anglo-Saxon ("Old English")	450 to 1100s
Middle English	1100s to late 1400s
Geoffrey Chaucer	1340(?)–1400
English Renaissance	late 14th–16th centuries
Queen Elizabeth's reign	1558–1603
William Shakespeare	1564–1616
English Restoration	1660
Queen Victoria's reign	1837–1901

FORGOTTEN

ENGLISH

1. The Animal Kingdom
Boanthropy, Scandaroons, and Cuckoo-Ales

BARNACLE-GOOSE * Name given to a species of wild goose (*Anas leucopsis*) for their supposed metamorphosis from barnacles. For centuries these "crustacean-birds," also known as *tree geese*, were commonly imagined to grow with their tiny beaks initially attached to seaside trees before dropping into the sea where they became mature geese. In the first written account of barnacle-geese in 1186, Giraldus Cambrensis reported that they

> . . . are produced from fir timber tossed along the sea and are at first like gum. Afterwards they hang down by their beaks as if they were seaweed attached to the timber and are surrounded by shells in order to grow more freely. Having thus in the process of time been clothed with a strong coat of feathers, they fly freely away into the air. . . . I have frequently seen with my own eyes, more than a thousand of these small birds, hanging down on the seashore from one piece of timber, enclosed in their shells and already formed.

For centuries, biological misconceptions such as this thrived, even among reliable writers like John Gerarde, who, in his 1597 *Herbal*, wrote convincingly—again from "first-hand observation"—of the barnacle-goose's life cycle, describing even the bird's size at maturity:

> When it is perfectly formed, the shell gapeth open, and the first thing that appeareth is the foresaid lace or string; next come the legs of the bird hanging out, and

as it groweth greater, it openeth the shell by degrees, till at length it is all come forth and hangeth only by the bill. In short space after it cometh to full maturity and falleth into the sea, where it gathereth feathers and groweth to a fowl bigger than a mallard and lesser than a goose.

Poets of the seventeenth century, such as Michael Drayton, found this mythological creature too appealing to resist as subject matter:

> Their roots so deeply soaked send from their stocky
>   boughs
> A soft and sappy gum, from which these tree-geese grow;
> Still great and greater thrive, until you well may see
> Them turned to perfect fowls; when dropping from the
>   tree
> Into the merry pond which under them doth lie,
> Wax ripe, and taking wing, away in flocks do fly.

In an attempt to capitalize on this freak of nature, an advertisement from a June 1807 newspaper informed readers of a barnacle-goose exhibition:

> The barnacles which form the present exhibit possess a neck upwards of two feet in length, resembling the windpipe of a chicken. Each shell contains five pieces, and not withstanding the thousands which hang to eight inches of the tree, part of the fowl may be seen from each shell.

From this fable of natural history was created the currently used scientific name *anatifera*, or "goose-bearing," as a classification for a type of barnacle.

BOANTHROPY * Rare form of insanity described in the nineteenth century, in which a man imagined himself to be the manifestation of an ox. The diagnosis of this madness was inspired by a passage from the Book of Daniel, in which King Nebuchadnezzar "was driven from men, and did eat grass as oxen, and his body was wet with the dew of heaven." A number of disorders could perhaps be classified as boanthropisms. Robert Chambers's 1864 work, *The Book of Days*, examined what he termed "ruminating men," including one gentleman

> . . . who actually chews the cud like an ox. He is apparently much like another tall stout man, but has many extraordinary properties, being eminent for strength, and possessing a set of ribs and sternum very surprising, and worthy the attention of anatomists. His body, upon the slightest touch, even through all his clothes, throws out electric sparks; he can reject his meals from his stomach at pleasure; and did absolutely, in the course of two hours, go through to oblige me, the whole operation of eating, masticating, swallowing, and returning by the mouth a large piece of bread and a peach. . . . I suppose his ruminating moments are spent in lamenting the peculiarities of his frame.

In another section, Chambers shared a story about a certain Anthony Recchi,

> who was obliged to retire from the dinner-table to ruminate undisturbed, and who declared that the second process of mastication "was sweeter than honey, and accompanied with a delightful relish." His son inherited the same faculty, but with him it was under better control, he being able to defer its exercise till a convenient opportunity.

Pasipae, the wife of King Minos of Crete, was said in mythology to have fallen in love with a bull, and even bore him a highly illegitimate son, as Samuel Butler noted in *Hudibras*, his ribald seventeenth-century satire directed against Puritans:

This made the beauteous queen of Crete
To take a town-bull for her sweet;
And from her greatness stoop so low,
To be the rival of a cow.

In 1792, Edward Jenner successfully developed a vaccine for smallpox by injecting a boy with closely related cowpox germs. He did this despite his medical critics' attempts to scuttle his project by circulating boanthropy scare-stories. The critics alleged that those inoculated would develop bovine appetites, make cowlike sounds, and go about on four legs butting people with their horns—either imagined or real ones. Other nine-

teenth-century doctors believed that the breath of a cow had beneficial effects for patients suffering from respiratory ailments such as tuberculosis, and sometimes prescribed living in lofts over cattle barns.

STALKING-HORSE * At least as early as the fifteenth century, this expression denoted a horse trained to graze as it slowly approached birds or other wild game. This clever camouflage often allowed its dismounted rider to come close enough to shoot his prey with bow and arrow, and later gun, from under the horse's belly or neck. Gervase Markham, in his 1621 *Hunger's Prevention*, described the stalking-horse as "Any old jade trayned up for that use, which . . . will gently . . . walke up and downe in the water. . . . You shall shelter your selfe and your [fowling] piece behind his fore shoulder." Markham also offered instructions for making the more convenient portable "blind," fashioned not only to resemble a horse but sometimes a cow or an ox, which eventually replaced its live predecessor: "In this case he may take any pieces of ould canvasse, and having made it in the shape and proportion of a horse . . . let it be painted as neere the colour as a horse as you can devise." Another figure employed as an animal-fooler, the Scottish *tulchane*, had a very different purpose. As found in John Jamieson's 1808 *Scottish Dictionary*, the tulchane consisted of "A calf's skin, in its rough state, stuffed with straw and set beside a cow to make her give milk." By the late sixteenth century, stalking-horse was used figuratively for a sneaky type of military maneuver, and by the early seventeenth century for an accomplice who, often unknowingly, assisted in underhanded ventures.

SCANDAROON * A pigeon, whose name was taken from the Turkish seaport Iskanderun. Native to North Africa, these birds were first used by an English trading post located in Iskanderun to alert traders of a vessel's impending arrival so they might prepare the docks for the receiving and loading of cargo. In the eighteenth century, this aerial messenger was trained by repeatedly carrying a mother bird out to sea, with her unfledged nestlings left behind, and releasing her from progressive distances to find her way home. A century earlier, Samuel Pepys had chronicled a homing exercise for pigeons used by an aristocratic acquaintance: ". . . carrying pigeons ten or twelve miles off and laying wagers which pigeon shall come home soonest." In the early 1700s, a century before carrier pigeons were formally domesticated and employed, we find poor Robinson Crusoe attempting the same training in his island habitat:

> I found a kind of wild pigeon in a tree. . . . And taking some young ones, I endeavored to breed them up tame, and did so; but when they grew older they flew all away, which, perhaps, was at first for want of feeding them, for I had nothing to give them.

In 1668, Pepys received an urgent summons to the house of a dying friend who had received the best of medical care: "So I to him, and find his breath in his throat; and they did lay pigeons to his feet. . . ." William Salmon, in his *Pharmacopeia Londinensis* of 1678, described a variation of this pigeon treatment, of special interest to doctors and psychotherapists: "And so laid to the head, takes away head aches, frenzy, melancholy and madness."

In his 1855 *Curiosities of London*, John Timbs described one of the dangers to these birds, despite the fact that killing or taking them was "an offense punishable summarily, by fine or imprisonment":

> Pigeon-poachers set traps to decoy their neighbors' pigeons, and it is calculated that we have in London upward of two thousand men thus graduating for the penal settlements. Hundreds of pigeon-traps are set on a Sunday morning; the gains are small, but the excitement is great, much artifice and patience being essential to success. At the utmost, a "green dragon" may produce two shillings or a "fine pouter" five shillings.

Financier Nathan Rothschild, by an early scandaroon-carried message, was among the first to learn of England's tide-turning victory over Napoleon in the Battle of Waterloo in 1815. Falsely hinting that the battle and therefore England's future was lost, he craftily manipulated the London stock market, causing share prices to tumble. He then cunningly bought up many artificially deflated securities, later reselling them at a huge profit. Because of Iskanderun's sordid reputation in the 1600s—not its association with Rothschild—scandaroon also came to denote a swindler.

———

FEAGUE ✳ Eighteenth-century verb meaning to administer to a horse a suppository made of raw ginger. This was a com-

mon practice among horse dealers, also called *chanters,* to make the horse livelier, to hide lameness of the hind legs, and to stimulate it to carry its tail better. Occasionally, a live eel was substituted for the ginger with unusually sluggish horses or when exaggerated results were desired. Apparently these tricks were employed so routinely that an eighteenth-century account stated, "A forfeit is incurred by any horse dealer's servant who shall show a horse without first feaging him." An 1863 self-help book of English legal advice listed fifty-six "defects and diseases . . . said to constitute unsoundness in horses," which should be considered before buying, including:

Glanders, farcy, "chink in the chine" [spinal problems, such as "sway back"], strangles, poll evil, grease, grogginess, Mallenders and Sallenders [leg afflictions], thick wind, roaring, gutta serena [glass eye], enlarged hock, founder [fever in the feet], nasal gleet, Sandcrack, and wind-sucking.

Thomas Dekker's 1608 *Lanthorn and Candlelight* explained how to hide a horse's runny nose, a telltale sign of "glanders":

In the very morning when he is to be rifled away amongst the gamesters in Smithfield . . . the horse-courser tickles his nose with a good quantity of the best [s]neezing powder that can be gotten, which with a quill being blown up into the nostrils to make it work the better, he stands poking there up and down with two long feathers plucked from the wing of a goose, they being dipped in the juice of garlic . . . to make the dumb beast void the filth from his nostrils, which he will do in great abundance. This being done, he comes to him with a new medicine for a sick horse, and mingling the juice of bruised garlic, sharp biting mustard, and strong ale together, into both nostrils with a horn is poured a good quantity of this filthy broth, [after] which . . . his nose will be cleaner than his master's . . . and the filth be so artificially stopped that for eight or ten hours, a jade will hold up his head with the proudest gelding that gallops scornfully by him, and never have need of whipping.

Another concern for a buyer was whether his horses were free of witchcraft, which John Aubry addressed in his 1695 *Miscellanies upon Various Subjects:*

Mr. S. told me that his horse, which was bewitched, would break bridles and strong halters, like Samson. They filled a bottle of the horse's urine, stopped it with a cork . . . and then buried it under the ground; and the party suspected to be the witch fell ill, that he could not make water, of which he died.

In *King Lear*, Shakespeare remarked of horse buyers: "He's mad that trusts in the tameness of a wolf, a horse's health, a boy's love or a whore's oath."

BAG-FOX ✳ A live fox bound in a cloth sack, supplied for the chase in eighteenth- and nineteenth-century England. Like many wild animals, foxes were long considered a general nuisance, but were imported from France and the Low Countries for "the chase," since their numbers had been so heavily reduced by farmers and hunters. Foxes could be crafty enough to elude the dogs and their pampered and often drunken aristocratic masters, so bag-foxes were sometimes released only after being doused with a pungent turpentine solution, as this eighteenth-century verse by John Wolcot testified:

> Thus the bag-fox, (how cruelly, alack!)
> Turned out with turpentine on his back,
> Amidst the war of hounds and hunters flies;
> Shows sport, but luckless by his fragrance dies.

These shy creatures were traded at London's Leadenhall Market, where local game was featured by purveyors called *Leadenhallers*. In his eighteenth-century journal, Gilbert White made an observation about foxes during mating season that raised the question why dogs, or hunters themselves, would need help in locating them: "Foxes begin now to be very rank, and to smell so high that as one rides along of a morning, it is easy to distinguish where they have been." In Shakespeare's *Twelfth Night*, this once familiar odor alluded to a devious plot so suspicious and obvious that only a simpleton "will cry upon't, for all this, though it be as rank as a fox." Victorian writer

Oscar Wilde fashioned this observation about the pastime of fox hunting: "The English country gentleman galloping after a fox—the unspeakable in full pursuit of the uneatable."

CRAPANDINA * Early sixteenth-century name for a mineral, also known as a *toad-stone* or *bufonite*, to which extraordinary, if perhaps ironic, healing properties were attributed. The stone was supposed to be a "natural concretion" found in the head of the common toad that acted as an antidote to poison.

Thomas Lupton, in his 1579 *A Thousand Notable Things*, described how "A toad-stone called crapandina, touching any part envenomed, hurt or stung, with rat, spider, waspe or any other venomous beast, ceases the paine or swelling thereof." He kindly informed his readers how to acquire this valuable stone:

> Put a great or overgrowne tode into an earthen potte, and put the same into an antes hyllocke, & cover the same with earth, which tode at length antes wyll eate, so that the bones of the toad and stone wyll be left in the potte.

Dried toads were once found in home medicine cabinets in Devonshire, to be used for such purposes as making the following dropsy recipe from Elizabeth Wright's 1914 *Rustic Speech and Folk-Lore:* "Take several large, fully-grown toads, place them in a vessel in which they can be burned without their ashes becoming mixed with any foreign matter." The odd belief in the efficacy of the crapandina is evident in the famous lines from Shakespeare's *As You Like It:*

> Sweet are the uses of adversity
> Which, like the toad, ugly and venomous
> Wears yet a precious jewel in his head.

BEE-MASTER * One who, into the late nineteenth century, tended hives and performed the essential task of informing

an estate's bees of important household events. Bees were long considered sacred in Britain, and a potential source of good fortune, and as such became like pets to rural families. A unique funerary custom involving these insects, once found throughout England, was described by E. M. Wright:

To "tell the bees" is to inform them of the occurrence of the death of the head of the house, or of some member of the family. If this is not done, they are supposed to leave their hives and never return, or else all die. The right time for making the communication is either just before the funeral leaves the house, or else at the moment when the procession is starting. On the Welsh border, people say it must be made in the middle of the night. The form of words used varies in different parts of the country, but they must always be whispered words, or the bees will take offence.

Hives were actually "put into mourning," with the attachment of black crepe, and failure to "tell the bees" in Devonshire could result in the death of a family member. This breach sometimes also had serious repercussions for the bees, as Chambers described:

> The bees seemed very sickly . . . when my neighbour's servant bethought him that they had never been put in mourning for their late master; on this he got a piece of crepe and tied it to a stick, which he fastened to the hive. After this the bees recovered.

In some places, sugar, beer, and bits of cakes or other refreshments served at the funeral were placed in a saucer before the hives, as we learn from J. Hardy's *Denham Tracts*. One man, he wrote, "had seen a piece of the funeral cake placed at the mouth of the hive, which the inmates dragged within with a 'mournful noise.' " George Williamson's 1923 *Curious Survivals* observed another type of obligatory ritual for the bee-master:

> He was just as punctilious about telling the bees of a wedding, and on the occasion of his granddaughter's wedding, brought her, after she had been married, to the bees, and announced the fact of her marriage to each hive in succession, and fastened on to each a tiny scrap of white

ribbon, which the bride kissed before she handed it to him, and which, he declared, would have no advantage or information to the bees, unless she herself had marked it in this way.

CUCKOO-ALE * Spontaneous annual celebration by laborers upon hearing the first song of a cuckoo, especially if they had money in their pockets, as that was a sure sign that they would not want for money again that year. However, if this first note was detected while in bed, bad luck was expected until the new year. The cuckoo, because of its habit of migrating between Wales and England, was nicknamed the *Welch-ambassador*, and has been considered a harbinger of spring in England from time immemorial. An ale specially brewed for this "holiday," also called cuckoo-ale, was drunk outdoors in honor of the expected change of season. Divination was practiced when the cuckoo was first detected, as the Lupton described in 1579:

> When you see the cuckoo, marke well where your right foote doth stande, for you shall fynd there an hair, which if it be black, it sygnifyes that you shall have very evyll lucke all that yeare after. If it be whyte, then very good lucke. But if it be graye, then indyfferent.

Because of its special technique of laying its eggs in other birds' nests, more than seven hundred years ago the cuckoo inspired early forms of *cuckold*, a man with an unfaithful wife. This derogatory name may have endured because at one time, husbands were warned of approaching male adulterers by men who made a sound like a cuckoo, which became associated with the victimized men. The Romans used a similar Latin word, *cuculus*, to indicate the adulteress, and called her husband a *carruca*, a hedge sparrow. *Wittol*, a term for a husband who was aware of but unbothered by his wife's indiscretions, was "from the wi-tewal, the green woodpecker, from the belief that it hatched the cuckoo's eggs and raised the young as its own." Reflecting changes in societal values, Somerset Maugham, in his preface to his collected twentieth-century plays, wrote, "I submit to my fellow dramatists that the unfaithfulness of a wife is no longer a subject for drama, but only for comedy." A Sussex folk rhyme highlighted a few of the cuckoo's strange habits:

> The cuckoo is a merry bird, she sings as she flies
> She brings us good tidings, she tells us no lies
> She dries up the dirt in the Spring of the year
> And sucks little birds' eggs to keep her voice clear.

The use of cuckoo as a synonym for crazy came from Gotham, an English village near Nottingham, renowned since the four-teenth century for being inhabited by fools. A plan was apparently developed there to form a hedge around one of these birds in order to permanently effect an idyllic springtime climate.

———

BUGGERY * An indelicate expression referring to sodomy involving animals, which seventeenth-century historian Edward Chamberlayne claimed was brought to England by the Roman Lombards. The term *bugger*, from which buggery was formed, was taken from a sect of eleventh-century Bulgarian wayfarers originally called *bougres* by the French. Corrupted to *bugger* in Middle Dutch and later borrowed by the English, bougres was used to distinguish other groups to whom these practices were ascribed, as well as usurers. For example, Nathaniel Bailey's 1749 dictionary offered a convenient but far-fetched explanation for the name, remarking that it was from the "Bulgari[ans], a people infamous for unnatural lust." Buggery was condemned as the action of a "heretike" as early as 1330, and in the 1550s, a decade after Henry VIII created his infamous *Ordinance against*

Buggerie, this newly categorized felony was transformed into a "decent" legal term. By 1754, the "unnatural behavior of buggery" was listed among the "most horrid crimes," along with adultery, murder, and blasphemy. Although buggery could be punished with death as late as the eighteenth century, flogging, banishment, and the pillory were more commonly employed. In 1861, a manuscript recorded a different aspect of buggery, describing "the abominable crime of buggery, committed either with mankind or with any animal." One unusual group of buggers, called *hippospadians* (*hippo* meant horse to the ancient Greeks, from Hippona, goddess of horses), were, according to Blount, "monstrous persons that abuse themselves with a horse. In February, 1652, one of these was convict[ed] . . . for being buggered by a horse and both she and the horse were burnt according to Mosaical Law."

2. *Physician, Heal Thyself*
Nimgimmers, Eagle-Stones, and Fleam

GARGARICE * Thirteenth-century Old French word for mouthwash, which might have contained any of the following ingredients: wine, pepper, honey, vinegar, camphor, *grayn de paradys* (cardamom), or other spices when available, especially rosemary, as in this description from Gerarde's *Herbal:*

> Rosemary comforteth the brain, the memory, and the inward senses. The distilled water of the flowers, being drunk morning and evening, taketh away the stench of the mouth and breath, and maketh it very sweet.

Gargarice was drawn from the same Latin source, *gargarismus*, as gargle, "to rattle in the throat," and *gargoyle*, the Gothic rooftop beast-sculptures that spout rain water from their mouths. *Gargarism* was depicted in 1656 by Blount as "A liquid potion to wash the mouth and throat which is not suffered to go down but to bubble up and down the throat." Tooth-soape, called *odontosmegma* in Robley Dunglison's 1844 *Medical Dictionary*, is mentioned by Edward Topsell's 1607 *History of Foure-Footed Beasts*, as a powder made

> . . . of the heads of mice being burned . . . for scouring and cleansing of the teeth, unto which if spikenard [lavender] be added or mingled, it will take away any filthy scent or strong savour in the mouth.

Nicholas Culpeper's *Herbal* explained a more wholistic "head-purge":

The head is purged by Gargarisms, of which Mustard, in my opinion, is excellent, and therefore a spoonful of Mustard put into the mouth, is excellent for one that is troubled with the lethargy; but be sure that if you would keep your brain clear, keep your stomach clean.

Cavities, once believed to be caused by worms, were plugged by medieval dentists—who were once called *tooth-carpenters*—with wood and lead, as well as copper, or silver filed from coins. In the eighteenth and nineteenth centuries, alloys with low melting temperatures were sometimes poured in while molten. Toothaches were also relieved by rubbing a dead mouse on the

cheek near the pain, or by using a hammer and nail, as we find in alchemist Sir Kenelm Digby's 1648 *Receipts:*

With an iron-nail . . . cut the gum from about the teeth till it bleed, and that some of the blood stick upon the nail; then drive it into a wooden beam. . . . After this . . . you never shall have the tooth-ach in all your life.

———————

NIMGIMMER * Seventeenth-century term for what Thomas Dyche's 1740 dictionary described as "A surgeon, or one

that cures the clap [venereal disease] or pox." Henri de Mondville, born in 1260, was one of the most noted nimgimmers of
his day and, we may infer from his writings, an early believer
in the power of positive thinking. He once advised an appren-
tice, "Keep your patients' spirits up with music [of] a 10-string
psalter, with letters about the deaths of his enemies or—if he
is a religious man—by telling him he's been made a bishop."
Mondville's methods seem in harmony with an assertion of Jonathan Swift, in *Polite Conversations*, that "The best doctors in
the world are Dr. Diet, Dr. Quiet and Dr. Merriman." It appears that the Roman physician Galen, who lived a thousand

years before Mondville, could well lay claim to having made
the first recorded attempts at attitudinal healing. His biogra-
phers indicate that Galen's many medical innovations, such as
taking patients' medical histories before treating them, included
telling patients amusing stories to improve their conditions.
Most nimgimmers overlooked the value of exercise, a notable
exception being Nicholas Andry, who in his 1743 book, *Orthopædia*, extolled its virtues—even for members of the vegetable kingdom:

> Exercise is so useful and necessary that not only man, but
> the most unactive and indolent of the brute creation, nay,

even plants themselves cannot thrive without it. The humble violet, as well as the mighty oak, loves to be agitated by winds.

PHRENOLOGIZE * Mid-nineteenth-century verb meaning to discover a person's traits by the bumps on his or her skull, based upon the study of *phrenology*. The meaning of this word was soon altered by detractors to a "blow to the head." One lampoon found in an 1848 issue of *Blackwell Magazine* satirically characterized a gentleman who "emerged with a broken hat and a head phrenologized by a blacking bottle." In 1858, J. W. Donaldson attacked the secular precepts of this "scullery science," saying of its founder, "He not only made the soul a mere function of the body, but even phrenologized it by placing it in the forehead."

Phrenology is descended from a much older, possibly French practice known as *physiognomy*, a word from Old French, Latin, and Greek sources, characterized in Randle Cotgrave's 1611 dictionary as "A guess at the nature, or inward disposition, by the features or outward lineaments [of the face]." In 1838, Joseph Morel de Rubempré published a compendium of "applied phrenology" articles written by practitioners that, when employed correctly with brass measuring calipers called "craniometers," would enable the mostly male readership to secretly assess women by "knowing their qualities, faults, characters, and perceiving their thoughts, desires, inclinations, secrets, tastes, passions, fidelity, indiscretions, etc." In 1844, a straightforward portrayal of this pseudoscience was published in Dunglison's mainstream, eight-hundred-page medical dictionary. About phrenology's synonym, *craniology*, or "craziology," as it was also known, and its related examination procedure called *cranioscopy*, he wrote: "They signify the description, or simply the examination of the external parts of the surface of the cranium, in order to deduce from thence a knowledge of the different intellectual and moral dispositions." He then listed twenty-seven "faculties," or "organs," found in phrenological teachings, including "amativeness" (lust), "venereal instinct," love of strife, "carnivorous instinct," cupidity,

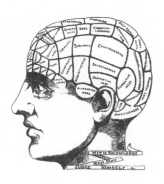

inclination to robbery, vanity, wit, and mimicry. He defined *cranomancy* as "The art of divining—from inspection of the head or cranium—the moral dispositions and inclinations of individuals."

Herman Melville was gently critical of this form of quackery, writing in *Moby Dick* about 1850:

> I consider that the phrenologists have omitted an important thing in not pushing their investigations from the cerebellum through the spinal canal. For I believe that much of a man's character will be found betokened in his backbone. . . . A thin joist of spine never yet upheld a full and noble soul.

The phrenological movement lasted into the 1920s in the United States, where its "bump doctors" were kept up to date by the *American Phrenological Journal*, a magazine hailed by its respected medical counterpart, the *Boston Medical and Surgical*

Journal, as "an excellent publication with which we could not
well dispense."

FLEAM ✳ Bloodletting instrument or lancet, whose name
dates back to at least the early 1500s. It was created from the
Greek root *phleb,* vein, which also serves as the root of the
modern word *phlebotomy.* The abandoned art of bleeding, which
can be traced to Roman times and farther back to Hippocrates,
was resurrected by studious and celibate medieval monks, who
initially bled one another as a means of reducing unwanted
sexual passions. This procedure was made palatable to the general public, on whom it was later used, by its promotion as a
form of disease treatment and prevention. Even aged and debilitated sixteenth- and seventeenth-century patients found
themselves subject to a modified form of prescribed blood loss,

mysteriously called *boxing,* as characterized by Philip Barrough's 1624 treatise, *Method of Physick:* "But if age or weakness
do prohibite bloud letting, you must use boxing, not to the
head itselfe, but to the parts adjoining, as the shoulders and
breaste, to pull backe the bloud." Barrough insisted that selecting the proper vein for each type of ailment was as critical

a consideration as fleam size: ". . . let bloud of the veine which is between the ring-finger and the eare-finger [little finger]." In his 1662 diary, Pepys suggested another rationale for bloodletting: "Mr. Holliard came to me and let my blood, about sixteen ounces, I being exceedingly full of blood."

Although his 1653 *London Dispensatory* is commonly referred to as the *Complete Herbal*, some of Nicholas Culpeper's prescriptions contained much more than herbal remedies:

> If the liver be too hot, it usually proceeds from too much blood, and is known by redness of the urine, the pulse is swift, the veins great and full [and] the spittle, mouth and tongue seem sweeter than they used to be; the cure is letting blood in the right arm.

A well-stocked home medicine cabinet of the eighteenth century often contained bleeding instruments for use in such odd procedures as the following, also from Culpeper: "When no other means will stop the bleeding at the nose, it has been known that it hath been stopped by opening a vein in the ear." Samuel Bayfield's 1832 treatise on the related art of *cupping*, which brought "bad blood" to the surface, included the following description:

> Hot water was first heated up and the cups immersed in it until they became warm. The part of the body to be cupped (near the site of the infection, or more generally behind the ears, the temple or the scalp) was "fomented" with hot water. The cupping vessel was placed on the part, and a wick from a burner placed under the glass for a second or two. As the burner used up or "exhausted" the air in the glass, the skin beneath the cupping glass rose slowly into the glass. . . . Bleeding was continued to the point of faintness, when the patient's skin had become pallid, the heart-beat reduced, fever cooled, and restlessness replaced with a shock-like state.

On December 26, the Feast Day of their patron Saint Stephen, horses were bled, frequently as a preventative measure, after being run "until they doe extremely sweate." This odd superstition was commented upon in Hugh Latimer's *Sermons* of 1555: "But I marvel how it came to passe that this day we were wont to let our horses blood. It is as though St. Stephen had some great government over the horses which, no doubt, is a vaine invention of man."

EAGLE-STONE * Hollow stone or fossil, first presented in Greek mythology, and later by the Roman historian Pliny as *aetites*, which produced a rattling sound when shaken because of a small bit of debris trapped inside. Pliny, however, offered the disclaimer that the eagle-stone "has no medical properties, however, except immediately after it has been taken from the nest." From the early 1400s, it was believed that eagles, in whose nearly inaccessible nests these objects were sometimes found, were unable to hatch or raise healthy offspring without them. Because of the "stone within a stone," these charms were also thought to have magical fertility properties for women that could ease and change the pace of delivery and even prevent miscarriage, along with prayers to Saint Carmenta.

In *Occult Miracles of Nature* of 1658, Levinus Lemnius reported of the eagle-stone that "It makes women that are slippery able to conceive, being bound to the left arm; being applied to the thigh of one that is in labour, makes a speedy and easy delivery, which thing I have found true by experiment." However, Lupton warned that birthing mothers had to be careful not to overemploy the eagle-stone: "This stone tyed to her thygh, brings an easie & lyght birth, but you must take it away quicklie after birth." The problem, according to *Aristotle's Midwife*, was that "Aetites, held to the privities . . . draws away both child and after burden, but great care must be taken to remove it presently or it will draw forth the womb and all."

The eagle-stone was mentioned in a 1751 edition of John Hill's *History of the Materia Medica* (*materia medica* refers to publications that for centuries have listed herbs and various substances with medical properties). It was also mentioned in the 1662 *Catalogue of Dr. Bargrave's Museum:*

> It is so useful that my wife can seldom keep it at home, and therefore she hath sewed the strings to the knit purse in which the stone is, for the convenience of the tying of it to the patient on occasion, and hath a box to put the purse and stone in. It were fit that . . . the Canterbury dean's . . . wife should have this stone in [her] custody for the public good.

An article from as late as 1862 suggested that eagle-stones also "possessed the singular property of detecting theft."

––––––––

TOAD-EATER ∗ Originally, a seventeenth-century charlatan's obedient sidekick who, in view of a crowd, would pretend to eat a toad, a creature then considered very poisonous. In response to this, the assistant would feign a severe reaction, to the horror and sometimes amusement of the naive spectators. The mountebank master, being careful *not* to invoke the name of Saint Benedict, the patron saint of poisoning victims, would then dramatically demonstrate the curative power of a remedy potion that he had for sale by "reviving" his sidekick. Butler commented upon the psychology used by these hucksters:

> Doubtless, the pleasure is as great
> Of being cheated as to cheat;
> As lookers-on feel most delight,
> That least perceive a juggler's slight,

And still the less they understand,
The more th' admire his slight of hand.

Toads once had many applications for the sick, including one mentioned in Salmon's 1678 *London Dispensary:* "Toad steept in vinegar . . . stops bleeding at nose, especially laid to the forehead . . . or hung about the neck." A corresponding verb based upon this common scenario, *toad-eat*, developed about this time. It meant to do something quite unpleasant for one's master and survived as the verb "toady."

The toxicity of toads was legendary. Thomas Lupton tells a supposedly true story of two lovers who both died suddenly from rubbing their teeth with leaves of sage, an early substitute for a toothbrush, at the base of which "was a greate toade founde, which infected the same with his venomous breath." Perhaps the most remarkable exaggeration to be found on toadal toxicity is from Samuel Purchas's 1625 work, *Pilgrimes*, regarding the legend of Sultan Cambay, who was said to have dined regularly upon various poisons, with toads being a favorite. In the story, the sultan created what Shakespeare called in *King John* "the vile prison of afflicted breath" by consuming these noxious substances, so that contact with him was said to have caused the death of four thousand of his concubines. Butler makes reference to this bizarre tale in *Hudibras*, adding mention of the asp, a small, poisonous snake, and the basilisk, an imaginary reptile hatched from a "cock's egg," whose breath and gaze were believed lethal:

> The Prince of Cambay's daily food
> Is asp, and basilisk and toad,
> Which makes him have so strong a breath,
> Each night he stinks a queen to death.

KINGSEVIL * Medical condition of the cervical lymph nodes, also known as *scrofula*, Latin for "a little pig." Scrofula alluded to the pig's practice of digging up balls of filth, which looked like the swellings found in a sufferer's neck. Until the eighteenth century, this infirmity was believed to be curable only by the touch of the ruling English or French monarch. The kings and queens were the people's link to God, and these swellings were considered a divine "visitation" to be counter-acted only by royalty. In *Macbeth*, the king's curious powers were glorified by Malcolm:

> 'Tis call'd the evil:
> A most miraculous work in this good king,
> Which often, since my here-remain in England,
> I have seen him do. How he solicits heaven,
> Himself best knows; but strangely-visited people,
> All swoln and ulcerous, pitiful to the eye,
> The mere dispair of surgery, he cures;
> Hanging a golden stamp about their necks,
> Put on with holy prayers.

In 1660, Pepys attended a session scheduled for Charles II: "To my lord's lodgings, and there staid to see the king touch people for the King's evil. But he did not come at all, it rayned so; and the poor people were forced to stand all the morning in the rain."

Dr. Andry prescribed for his patients the earliest possible preventative measure for this problem:

> As to the King's-Evil, you must, if possible, begin to use means against it, as soon as the child is born, by provid-ing him with a nurse whose milk, besides the other gen-eral qualities which good milk ought to have, is not too old; for if it is old, it must be too thick, and by this

thickness, occasion obstructions and disorders in the blood, which will readily fall upon the glands of the neck and consequently dispose the child to the King's-Evil.

Henri Misson's 1719 *Travels in England* outlined the transmission of the king's "healing energy" during the ceremony, but raised some doubts concerning the credibility of this treatment:

> When the king was weary of . . . touching the cheek or chin, Father Peter, the almoner, presented him with the end of the string which was round the patient's neck. The virtue pass'd from the hand to the string, from the string to the cloaths, from the cloaths to the skin, to the root of the evil. After this royal touch, those that were really ill were put into the hands of the physicians; and those that came only for the medal had no need of other remedies.

In 1684, English chronicler John Evelyn reported on the popularity of these healing events: "There was so grette and eager a concourse of people with their children to be touched of the evil that six or seven were crushed to death by pressing at the chirurgeon's door for tickets."

Charles II was said to have touched a hundred thousand subjects, who came with a variety of infirmities during his reign (more than eight thousand in 1662 alone), though the number of remissions produced, if any, was not recorded. Colorful John Aubrey, in his 1695 *Miscellanies upon Various Subjects*, reported that a man named "Evans had a fungous nose and said, it was revealed to him, that the king's hand would cure him. At the first coming of Charles II into St. James' Park, he kissed the king's hand and rubbed his nose with it, which disturbed the king but cured the nose." William III was rightfully skeptical about his role as healer and was induced to touch only a single sufferer, whom he advised, "God give you better health and more sense." The last monarch to perform this function was Queen Anne in 1714, who reportedly had touched the young Samuel Johnson two years earlier "without effecting a cure."

PISMIRE * Used as early as 1385 by Geoffrey Chaucer, this term signified the common ant, which was simply called a *mire* in Middle English. Pismire's prefix referred to the smell of urine that was once believed to mysteriously emanate from anthills, a clue to which involved a medical test employed by Roman physicians. In this procedure, a patient's urine was dripped near an anthill; if a high sugar content was present in the urine, ants would be attracted to it and diabetes was the likely cause. This possibly accurate evaluation lead to the vulgar appellation *piss-prophet*, applied to seventeenth-century diagnosticians who employed either this procedure or the more direct alternative— tasting the samples themselves. Shakespeare held these "watercasters" in low esteem, as is evident from this line at their expense from *Henry IV*, where Falstaff's page gives him the news about his "water evaluation": "He said, sir, the water itself was a good healthy water; but, for the party that owned it, he might have more diseases than he knew for."

Children's urinary problems, such as bedwetting, or nocturnal *watergate* in Old Scottish, were addressed in the sixteenth century by the addition of a goat bladder or goat droppings, dried to a powder, to a glass of wine. Another, from Eliza Smith's 1758 *Compleat Housewife*, recommended: "In a quart of beer, boil a handful of the berries of elegantine till it becomes a quart; drink it off luke-warm." Two hundred years ago, a home remedy said "to give ease in fits of the [kidney] stone, and to cure the suppression of urine," was prepared as follows:

> Take snail-shells and bees, of each an equal quantity; dry
> them in an oven with a moderate heat; then beat them

to a very fine powder, of which give as much as will lie on a sixpence, in a quarter of a pint of bean-flower water, every morning, fasting two hours after it; continue this for three days together. This has been found to break the stone and to force a speedy passage of urine.

Topsell's *History of Foure-footed Beastes* recommended: "Sodden [boiled] mice are exceeding good to restraine and hold in the urine of infants or children being too aboundant, if they be given in some pleasant or delightsome drinke." Lupton, a few years earlier, confidently touted a similar cure: "A flayne mouse, rosted or made in powder & drunk at one tyme, doeth

perfectly helpe such as can not holde or keepe their water, especially if it be used three dayes in this order. This is verie true and often proved."

AURUM POTABILE ✳ Literally "drinkable gold," borrowed directly from Latin around the seventeenth century. Aurum potabile seems to have been a variant of the age-old "gold fever" syndrome, when doctors considered this potentially toxic metal a panacea for many physical ailments. It was even considered "an antidote for poverty—a sickness very catching." Aurum potabile was only one of a number of potions which included minute particles of the yellow metal suspended in a "blood-red, hony-like" liquor, described in Elias Ashmole's 1650 *Chymical Collections* as a "golden oyle, a medicine most mervelous to preserve man's health." Gold was used in a variety of ways, including as a coating for pills dispensed to wealthy patrons with easily offended palates. This expensive process, called *de-auration*, was defined in Dyche's 1740 dictionary as "The covering with gold, as apothecaries do their pills, to prevent the nauseous taste of their physick being irksome to the patient."

John Hall, a physician and husband of Shakespeare's only daughter, commended gold's use through patient testimonials

in *Select Observations on English Bodies*, case records of two hundred of his patients. In the history of a woman under his care, he noted a detailed prescription or recipe for a certain pill "made five of a drachm, covered with gold," and added, "By the use of this [regimen] she gained strength very much and said it was as good as Aurum potabile, and would never be without it." Aubrey, in his 1686 *Remains of Gentilisme*, wrote about gold's use in healing:

Some doe use pure gold bound to old ulcers and fistulas as a secret, and with good success. Gold attracts mercury, and I have a conceit that the curing of ye kings evil by gold was first derived from hence. But the old gold was very pure and printed with St. Michael the Arch-angel, & to be stamped according to some rule astrological.

The Compleat Housewife contained "a powder for convulsion-fits," which required that oak-mistletoe and "five leaves of gold," along with several other herbs, be powdered and served in "a spoonful of black cherry-water, or if you please, *hysteric-water.*"

LETTICE-CAP ✳ Sixteenth-to seventeenth-century medical appliance resembling a hair net, used to treat a myriad of bodily disorders, including headaches and insomnia. In this net

was placed a variety of herbal materials—though probably not lettuce—often directly touching a patient's specially shaved head, as these lines (spoken by a physician in one of Beaumont and Fletcher's plays) illustrate:

> Bring in the lettice-cap. You must be shaved, sir.
> And then how suddenly we'll make you sleep.

Another piece of headgear prescribed by seventeenth-century physicians was called a *cucupha*, into which "curative" herbs, spices, or other materials were sewn. This device was worn during the 1600s as a remedy for a headache, a malady known by the Anglo-Saxons as a *head-weore* (literally "head weary"), which originated from a sense of hardship or grief. A related prophylactic tool, which survived well into Victorian times, involved the use of "snake-slough": "Get the skin of the viper and sew it into the lining of the hat. . . . People would hunt many miles for these skins in the month of April when the vipers shot their skin."

For churchgoers at Tellisford Cross, Somersetshire, the following headache treatment was said in a 1536 letter by John London to "have great virtue":

> In the body of the churche . . . wasse an image at an altar's end called Mayden Cutbrogh, and under her feet was a trowgh of wodde descending under the altar which wasse hollow. There resortyd such as wer trobelyd with the hedde ache. . . . Ther must they putt in to the trowgh a peck of oots, slydyd under the altar; the Crosse Fryers schuld behynd the altar privily stele them owt . . . and the sykk person schuld ak no more till the next time.

A less radical remedy "for an inveterate head-ach" was to

> Take the juice of the ground-ivy, and snuff it up the nose; it not only easeth the most violent head-ach for the present, but taketh it quite away. This cured one that had been afflicted with it many years, and by that use of it . . . it never returned.

The modern word *migraine* was borrowed and corrupted from an Old French word, *megrim*, which not surprisingly meant "foul mood," and was naturalized into English about 1400.

TEREBINTH * A tree from which turpentine was extracted, described by John Trevisa about 1400 as "a tre that sweteth rosine." Turpentine's use for medical purposes is well-documented, including Blount's account of its being

> put into ointments and emplaisters, for it glews, cleanses and heals wounds. It may be licked in [consumed] with honey and then it cleanses the breast and gently looseth the belly, provoking urine and driving out the [kidney] stone and gravel.

Pepys concluded his 1664 diary thinking about his good health: "But I am at a great losse to know whether it be [from] my hare's foot, or taking every morning of a pill of turpentine, or having left off the wearing of a gowne." The original 1771 version of the *Encyclopedia Britannica* promoted turpentine:

> The uses of turpentine in medicine are innumerable. It is . . . very detergent, and as such is prescribed in abscesses, ulcerations, etc. It promotes expectoration . . . and is most famous for clearing urinary passages. To be good, it must be clear and pellucid as water, of a strong penetrating smell and very inflammable.

Robert Hunter's *Encyclopedic Dictionary* of 1894 added to understanding of turpentine's versatility: "It is generally administered as an enema . . . in the intestines." Dyche's dictionary gave several additional applications of turpentine, including use

> . . . as a balsam to cuts and other green wounds, and taken inwardly is diuretick, occasioning the urine to smell like violets; boiled in water it becomes solid, and being so prepared is made into pills and given in venereal cases; the oil is used to consolidate wounds . . . and to strengthen the nerves.

On scurvy, John Bristowe's 1878 *Treatise on the Practice of Medicine* reported: "Among the remedies . . . recommended are lead, arsenic, digitalis, turpentine." The sixteenth-century proverb "Desperate diseases must have desperate remedies" seems to have been created with turpentine in mind.

GLISTER * A medical treatment defined by Bailey's dictionary as "fluid medicine of different qualities to be injected into the bowels." The term *clyster*, of which the sixteenth- to eighteenth-century glister was a variant, was itself a descendant of the Latin *cluere*, and ultimately the Greek *klyzein*, both meaning "to wash." By 1590, glister was being used figuratively, as in Greene's *Mourning Garment*, when he wrote of his finances, "My purse began with so many purging glisters to waxe not only laxative but quite empty." France's Louis XIV is known to have undergone as many as two thousand glisters, many while giving audience to members of his court or other visitors. A procedure found in an eighteenth-century medical book described "a clyster for the worms":

> Take of rue, wormwood [and] lavender cotton, three or four sprigs of each; a spoonful of aniseeds bruised; boil these in a pint of milk, let the third part be consumed; then strain it out and add to it as much aloes, finely powdered, as will lie on a three-pence; sweeten it with honey and give it pretty warm. It should be given three mornings together, and the best time is three days before the new or full moon.

Huskanoy, a term borrowed from Virginia Indians, involved subjecting an initiate to tribal ceremonies that included severe physical ordeals and colonic irrigations. In 1788, Thomas Jefferson wrote of someone who looked "so much out of his element that he has the air of one huskanoyed."

Hippocrates, the Greek "Father of Medicine," reportedly learned to administer glisters by observing the ibis, a sacred Egyptian wading bird, which he believed gave itself saltwater enemas with its long, curved bill when sick, as we learn from Blount:

> The use hereof was first learned from a bird in Ægypt called ibis, much like a storke, which bird doth often with her bill, open her hinder parts, when nature of her self doth not expel what is needful.

Shakespeare created a humorous double-entendre in his *Merchant of Venice*, when he had the Prince of Morocco deliver the adage: "All that glisters is not gold."

3. The Spirit World

Spoorns, Moone-Calves, and Night-Hags

SUCCUBUS * Mythical female fiend believed to explain the phenomenon of erotic dreams in medieval men. This word, derived from the Latin *succubare*, "to lie beneath," appears to be related to *succube*, a Late Latin term for a prostitute, and probably influenced the development of *succumb*. Of the succubus, Blount wrote:

> . . . the physitians affirm it to be a natural disease caused by humours undigested in the stomach, which fuming up to the brain, do trouble the animal spirits, stopping their passage into sinews so that the body cannot move.

This demon's male counterpart was the *incubus*, who was thought to descend and lie upon female sleepers of the fourteenth to eighteenth centuries for the purpose of carnal fulfillment. Like the succubus, his name referred to a sexual position, but in his case meant "to lie *upon*." So widespread was the reputation of these two that civil and ecclesiastical laws of the time referred to them by name. Sprenger and Kramer's fifteenth-century treatise, *Malleus Maleficarum*, even tackled the sticky question whether the devil could cause pregnancy through incubi: "It may be argued that devils take part in this generation . . . since they busy themselves by interfering with the process of normal copulation and conception by obtaining human semen and themselves transferring it."

As late as 1898, Dr. Foote's *Plain Home Talk*, a compendium of Victorian medical commentary on common conditions, took a dim view of amorous dreams:

Women, as well as men, are subject to these, and they are nearly as debilitating to the former as they are to the latter. Although no very vital secretions are lost by a woman so affected, the vital or nervous forces are expended without recompense . . . [and] is indeed practically an involuntary act of masturbation.

The word *incubation*, a bird's act of hatching eggs by sitting on them, is another linguistic link to these dreams of long ago.

TUT * General term applied to any fancied supernatural being, of which there were an abundance in the British Isles. Thomas Wright's 1857 provincial dictionary pointed out that "children are frightened by being told of Tom-tut, and persons in a state of panic . . . are said to be tut-gotten." The Latinesque *tutivillus*, from which tut can be traced, was also used by writers to bring forth images of a demon. E. M. Wright distinguished a variety of these fanciful English spooks, including two water-spirits from Yorkshire, Cheshire, and Durham named *Jenny Green-teeth* and *Nelly Long-arms*:

> . . . the various names of a nymph or water-demon who is said to lurk at the bottom of deep pits, ponds and wells. When children approach too near to the edge of her domain, she will stretch out her long, sinewy arms, seize them and drag them under water, holding them there till they are drowned. Her presence is indicated by a green scum on the surface of the water. If there is no pond or deep water near by, she has been supposed to take up a temporary lodging in the tops of trees, where after nightfall she may be heard moaning like the sighing of the night-wind through the branches of the trees. In some parts of the country, instead of Jenny Green-teeth, the boggart of the ponds is a masculine water-demon called Rawhead.

Wright also presented a glimpse of *Peg-a-lantern*, a malevolent lantern-bearing sprite. Peg haunted bogs and swampy meadows, where she gamboled and danced by herself or, when mischievously inspired,

> Hovering and blazing with delusive light,
> Misleads th'amaz'd night-wanderer from his way
> To bogs and mires, and oft through pond or pool,
> There swallow'd up and lost, from succor far.

Another tut, perhaps created to help people rationalize drowning, was called the *Water-Cow*. We learn from Jamieson about this amorphous Scottish spirit—remembered for its deep, long, "lowing" sound—whose dastardly malefactions resembled those of Jenny, Nelly, and Peg:

> The Water-Cow, in former times, haunted St. Mary's Loch . . . and though rather less terrible and malignant than the Water-Horse, yet, like him she possessed the rare slight of turning herself into whatever shape she pleased, and was likewise desirous of getting as many dragged into the lake as possible.

W. C. Hazlitt mentioned another tutivillus, called *Sherwl While*,

> . . . an evil spirit of the female sex, which . . . molested and misled any traveller. . . . She was accustomed when she saw anyone who had missed the road over the mountain, to greet him with, 'Whoop, whoop,' and to beckon him from a distance to follow her; she would then lead her dupe a long distance and end by bringing him back to the starting place.

In his *Agricultural Survey*, Kincard described the Scottish *doolie:* "This malign spirit, like the Water-Kelpie . . . was wont to haunt the fords and bridges, where he was particularly officious in inveigling the unwary traveller to take the most perilous tract."

BONE-FIRE * Summer pagan ritual in which animal bones were burned, originally to frighten off spirits, goblins, and unusual phantoms called *spoorns*, who were thought to roam at that time. This large outdoor ceremony became associated with Saint John's Eve (June 23) and Saint Peter's Eve (June 28) during the Middle Ages, and with the burning of saint's-bone relics and Bibles during Henry VIII's reign. In more rural areas, Torreblanca's *Demonology* reported, "The ancients were accustomed to pass their children of both sexes through the fire for the sake of securing them a prosperous and fortunate lot." A

correspondent for *Gentleman's Magazine* of February 1795 witnessed these sinister-looking activities on Midsummer's Eve in 1782, in Ireland:

> Exactly at midnight, the fires began to appear, and, going up to the leads of the house, which had a widely extended view, I saw on a radius of thirty miles all around, the fires burning on every eminence. I learned from undoubted authority that the people dance round the fires, and at the close went through these fires, and made their sons and daughters, together with their cattle, pass the

fire, and the whole was conducted with religious solemnity.

Bone-fires made their way inside the gates of London, where they became a popular year-round event, as we learn from Pepys's ironic diary entry of June 6, 1666, just three months before the devastating fire: "Bonefires were lighted all over towne. The joy of the city was this night exceeding great." As late as 1813, Brand's *Popular Antiquities* informed the reader that this custom was still alive: "Bonfires are still made on Midsummer Eve, in the northern parts of England and in Wales." As the fear of plague, witches, and subversive writings dwindled, bonfire, as the word came to be spelled, was tempered to mean simply any controlled, open-air blaze used to incinerate debris.

LYCANTHROPE * One who suffered the witchcraft-induced delusion of being a wolf. This grotesquely intriguing affliction was represented by Blount's seventeenth-century *Glossographia* as "frenzy or melancholly wherewith some being haunted, think themselves turned into wolves, fly the company of men and hide themselves in caves and holes, howling like wolves." Lycanthrope is descended from the Greek words *lykos*,

wolf, and *anthropos*, man, and translates from the Icelandic language as "going on a wolf's ride." Robert Burton's 1621 *Anatomy of Melancholy* commented: "Lycanthropia . . . or wolf-madness, when men run howling about graves and fields in the night and will not be pursuaded but that they are wolves, or some such beasts."

The concept of a wolf-man has a long history, extending back at least to classical Greek times when Herodotus first wrote of such a creature. The Romans had their own versions, including one presented by the poet Ovid as King Lycaon, who was transformed into a wolf-man for putting Jupiter's divinity to the test. The historian Pliny recorded that a Roman family, for some obscure reason, chose a member each year to assume a wolflike form that lasted for nine years. Saint Patrick was also believed to have turned Vereticus, King of Wales, into a wolf. A variation of this weird custom was delineated in William Baldwin's sixteenth-century treatise, *Beware the Cat:*

> There is also in Ireland one nacion whereof some one man and woman are at every seven yeeres end turned into wulves, and so continew in the woods the space of seven yeers; and if they happen to live out the time, they return to their own form again . . . and that this is true witnessed a man whom I left alive in Ireland, who had performed this seven yeeres penance, whose wife was slain while she was a wulf in her last yeer.

In most recorded cases, these beasts had wolfish appetites for humans and sought their prey after dark. They were usually of superhuman strength and, from medieval times could resist most weapons except those blessed in a church dedicated by Saint Hubert, patron saint of hunters.

ASTROLOGAMAGE ✳ A "wise man," or seventeenth-century *wizard*, who predicted events based upon celestial influences, as found in *Hudibras:*

> And men still grope t' anticipate
> The cabinet designs of Fate;
> Apply to wizards to foresee
> What shall and what shall never be.

These soothsayers often used their own secret symbols, formulas, and "mathematics" to come up with predictions and pronouncements. Though sometimes rivaling the Church in popularity among the lower classes, they were often viewed

with skepticism by many intellectuals such as Dante, who, in his *Inferno*, depicted them in hell with their heads turned so that they looked and walked backward. Other critics debunked them more directly, such as Erasmus, who in the sixteenth century wrote in *The Praise of Folly*,

> To this philosophical brotherhood belong all those who give out that they can foretell future events by observing the positions of the stars. And they predict the occur-

rences of the most prodigious proportions. Talk of marvels of magic! Why, they dwindle to insignificance when compared with the astounding wonders which astrologers declare to us are about to be. Yet—fortunate men—they find gullible people enough in the world to swallow their wildest announcements.

If expectant medieval parents were sufficiently affluent, a practitioner of this craft was normally present at the birth of their baby along with a midwife, though doctors and men in general were usually prohibited. Lancashire astrologamages, like those of other locales, often engaged in a variety of additional services, as we learn from Harland:

> Such a person usually combines the practice of Astrology with his other avocations. He casts nativities, gives advice respecting stolen property, tells fortunes and writes out charms for the protection of those who may consult him. . . . Even the wives of clergymen have been known to consult wise men on doubtful matters.

Time of day was one of the parameters used for predictions, Harland continued:

> All children that are born in the twilight of certain days are in consequence supposed to be endowed with the faculty of seeing spirits; and some of our "wise men" take advantage of this, and persuade their dupes that they were so circumstanced at birth.

These methods of divination appear comfortably civilized compared with a Scotch-Irish form known by the Gaelic name of *taghairm*, as we learn from Jamieson:

> A person was wrapped up in the skin of a newly slain bullock and deposited beside a water-fall, or at the bottom of a precipice, or some other strange, wild and unusual situation, where the scenery around him suggested

nothing but objects of horror. In this situation, he revolved in his mind the question proposed, and whatever was impressed upon him by his exalted imagination passed for the inspiration of the disembodied Spirits, who haunt their desolate recesses.

MOONE-CALFE * An animal monster, such as Shakespeare's Caliban from *The Tempest*, or a cow's fetus, once believed to have developed only into a shapeless lump, and literally "licked into shape" by its mother. Applied to adoles-

cents and adults during the 1600s, moone-calfe might have indicated a congenital idiot or an absent-minded or immature person, although it could also denote a monster deformed by lunar or demonic influences, perhaps as a result of the failure to take certain precautions outlined in this account of 1621: "When thou goest to thy bed . . . draw close the curtaines to shut out the Moone-light, which is very offensive & hurtfull to the braine, especially to those that sleepe." The Old English root, *cealf*, of which the word calf (of the leg) is a modern remnant, referred to a "swelling of flesh," or an improperly developed fetus, and according to Blount "makes women beleeve they are with child when they are not." Elizabethan gypsies attracted the related nickname "moon-men" because they were considered mad and inconstant, their reputations ranging from benign sages one moment to common thieves the next. The term *moon-silly* identified one who was smitten according to lunar influences, as Juliet warned Romeo in their famous balcony scene:

> O! Swear not by the moon, the inconstant moon,
> That monthly changes in her circled orb,
> Lest thy love prove likewise variable.

The eyes were thought to be stricken by the fluctuating lunar cycle—temporary blindness was known as *moon eye*, a phrase that also denoted eyes extraordinarily wide open because of fear. Admiral William Smyth's 1867 *Sailor's Word-book* contains the entry *moon-struck*, still heard today, which meant then "An influence imputed by the moon . . . by which fish . . . spoiled." Two centuries earlier, Milton had written of the moon's effects in *Paradise Lost:* "All maladies of ghastly spasm, or racking torture . . . moaping melancholie and moon-struck madness." The famous nineteenth-century Englishman David Livingstone, however, writing in his *Missionary Travels*, tried to downplay this notion of the moon's power: "You may sleep out at night, looking up to the moon till you fall asleep, without a thought or sign of moon-blindness."

NIGHT-HAG * A female demon who supposedly abducted people at night on horseback during the seventeenth to nineteenth centuries. It was believed that she created bad dreams in her victims by producing a feeling of suffocation, as we learn from Barrough's 1624 *Method of Physick:* "It is a disease, which as one thinketh himselfe in the night to be oppressed with a great weight, and beleeveth that something cometh upon him." Blount echoed this explanation, calling the nightmare—a

term generated from *mara*, an incubus (see *Succubus*, page 36)—
"a disease that troubles one so in sleep that he can scarce fetch
his breath." Shakespeare added a play on words in this passage
from *Romeo and Juliet:*

> This is the hag, when maids lie on their backs,
> That presses them and learns them to bear,
> Making them women of good carriage.

The nightmare was counteracted by placing one's shoes with
the toes pointing outward under the bed before retiring. Another method involved *holy bread*, blessed in local parish

churches. It was placed under a child's pillow at bedtime, as it
was believed to chase away evil spirits such as night-hags. This
belief is found in Herrick's *Hesperides:*

> Bring the Holy crust of bread,
> Lay it underneath the Head,
> 'Tis a charm to keep,
> Hags away while children sleep.

Until almost the fifteenth century, *hag-stones*, naturally perfo-
rated flint chips, were hung around bedposts or in stables in
rural England to prevent sleepless evenings, "be it man, woman

or horse," due to nightmares, as delineated in Aubrey's *Miscellanies:*

> To hinder the Night-mare, they hang on a string, a flint with a hole in it by the manger; but best of all they say, hung about their necks. That is to prevent the Nightmare, that is the hag, from riding their horses, who otherwise will sweat all night.

Thomas Blundevill, in 1566, wrote of this cure:

> A disease ["nightmare"] oppressing eyther man or beast, in the nighte season . . . an olde English wryter . . . teacheth howe to cure it with a fonde foolish charme, which bicause it perhappes make you gentle reader to laugh, as well as it did me . . . will rehearse it. Take a Flynt Stone that hath a hole of his owne kynde, and hang it over hym.

Hag-knots, an old term for matted snarls in a horse's mane, were supposedly used by witches as stirrups during evening flights. Into the twentieth century in Somerset, E. M. Wright wrote, "When horses break out into a sweat in the stable, they are said to be *hag-rided.*" Herrick's short poem, *Another Charme for Stables*, further illustrates this:

> Hang up hooks and shears to scare
> Hence the hag, that rides the mare,
> Till they be all over wet
> With the mire, and the sweat;
> This observ'd, the manes shall be
> Of your horses, all knot-free.

The *day-mare* was a later variation of nightmare, which brought unpleasant daytime thoughts.

MANDRAGORE * An archaic name for the mandrake, a plant with medical and supposed magical properties, which was reputed to cry out when cut. This trait is illustrated by lines from *Romeo and Juliet:*

> And shrieks, like mandrakes torn out of the earth,
> That living mortals hearing them run mad.

Ironically, this herb was used as a potent but risky anesthesia, often served in wine during medieval times. It was said by a nineteenth-century materia medica to have been "used when they wanted a narcotic of the most powerful kind." As John Donne portrayed in his 1610 *Pseudo-Martyr*, the character Annibal "mingled their wine with Mandrake, whose operation is betwixt sleepe and poyson." Lute wrote in his 1578 translation of *Dodoens*, "It is most dangerous to receive into the body the juice of the roote of this herbe, for if one take never so little more in quantitie than the just proportion . . . it cause[th] deadly sleepe and peevish drowsiness, like opium." This root, because of its handlike shape, was considered to be a powerful charm called the *main de gloire* (literally "hand of glory"), and "formed a staple article of belief among housebreakers in many parts of France, Germany, and Spain," as found in Grose's translation of *The Secrets of Little Albert:* "The use of the Hand of Glory was to stupefy those to whom it was presented, and to render them motionless insomuch as they could not stir any more than if they were dead." In his 1656 *Art of Simpling*, Coles noted that witches, performing a procedure with the mandragore that is now associated with voodoo, "Take likewise the roots of mandrake . . . and make thereof an ugly image by which they represent the person on whom they intend to exercise their witchcraft." In earlier times, it was believed that this root—and later the smoke-dried hand of an executed man, which was also called a "hand of glory"—when buried with gold or other precious metals would double their mass.

NEIDFYRE * Old English word for a fire ceremonially generated by intense friction between two pieces of wood. The purpose of these fires, which were employed well into the 1800s, was to counteract curses called *blastings*, placed upon livestock by malevolent witches or sorcerers. E. M. Wright wrote of another form of heat used to fortify liquids against spells: "A red-hot iron thrust into the cream in the churn, or into the fermenting beer in the brewing-vat expelled the witch that was frustrating the labours of the dairy-maid or the brewer." Jamieson reported on a Scottish treatment for "black spaul":

> When the cattle of any district were seized with this fatal distemper, the method of cure or prevention was to extinguish all domestic fires and rekindle them by "forced fire," caught from sparks emitted from the axel of the great wool-wheel, which was driven furiously round by the people assembled.

Once the villain was discovered, blood was taken from cattle suffering from *cowquake* or other afflictions and boiled, causing the witch personal discomfort, until the spell was removed. From the seventeenth to the nineteenth century, *need-fire* was a preventative ritual for ensuring the health of cattle, as this additional advice from Scot indicated:

> At Easter, you must take certain drops that lie uppermost of the holy Paschal candle, and make a little wax candle thereof; and upon some Sunday morning light it and hold it so as it may drop upon and between the horns and ears of the beast . . . and that which is left, stick it cross-wise

about the stable . . . and for all that year your cattle shall never be bewitched.

In his 1843 work, *The Doctor*, Robert Southey wrote of another witch-related farmers' scourge:

Concerning the kill-crops, as the Anglo-Saxons call them, whom the devil leaves in exchange when he steals children, for the purposes best known to himself. In Saxonia, near unto Halberstad was a man that also had a kill-crop who sucked the mother and five other women dry, and besides devoured very much.

The term *blasting* was derived from the Saxon verb *blastan*, "to spoil the fruits of the earth," and was used from the sixteenth to nineteenth centuries to describe, according to *Bailey's Dictionary*, "the sudden unexplainable damage to animals or crops [caused by] winds and frosts that immediately follow rain." Culpeper recommended the following conservative treatment "for eyes that are *blasted*": "Only wear a piece of black Sarcenet before thy eyes, and meddle with no medicine; only forbear wine and strong drink." An eighteenth-century "Ointment for a Blast" was prepared in the following manner:

Take velvet-leaves, wipe them clean, chop them small, put them to unsalted butter out of the churn, and boil them gently till they are crisp; then strain into a gallipot and keep it for use. Lay velvet-leaves over the part, after it is anointed.

This usage can still be heard in angry statements such as "this blasted toothache."

———

BROWNIES * Domestically inclined fairies, who were believed to perform household chores especially for farmers' families while they slept. The brownie, a close relative of England's

Robin Goodfellow, was perhaps named after the spirit Bawsey Brown, from the sixteenth-century Scottish poem *Dance of the Seven Deadly Sins*. The name may also have been influenced by their weatherbeaten skin, which according to Thomas Ruddiman's 1710 glossary was supposedly "swarthy or tawney colour, as those who move in a higher sphere are called fairies, from their fairness." In the late eighteenth century, John Brand remarked in his *Description of Zetland*,

> Not above forty or fifty years ago, almost every family had a brouny or . . . spirit which served them, to which they gave a sacrifice for his service, as when they churned their milk, they took a part thereof and sprinkled every corner of the house with it for Brounie's use. Likewise, when they brewed, they had a stone which they called Brounies Stane, wherein there was a little hole into which they poured some wort [partially completed beer] for a sacrifice.

John Milton wrote of the "wee brown men" around 1670 in *Allegro:*

> Tell us how the dredging Goblin swet,
> To earn his cream bowl duly set,
> When in one night 'ere glimpse of morn,
> His shadowy flale hath thrash'd the corn
> That ten day-lab'rers could not end;
> Then lays them down the lubbar-fiend,
> And crop-full out of doors he flings,
> Ere the first cock his matin rings.

This legend was summarized by an account in Jamieson's *Scottish Dictionary:*

> The brownie was meagre, shaggy and wild in appearance. In the day time he lurked in remote recesses of the old houses which he delighted to haunt; and in the night,

sedulously employed himself in discharging any laborious task which he thought might be acceptable to the family to whose service he had devoted himself. Although, like Milton's lubbar-fiend, he loves to stretch himself by the fire, [and] does not drudge from the hope of recompense.

These benevolent drudgery-doers served as a model for junior Girl Scouts, or "Brownies," who parents eagerly hoped would become enamored with doing housework.

4. *Let the Punishment Fit the Crime*

Ambodexters, Petty-foggers, and Usufruct

PIEPOWDER ✳ Along with its anglicized nickname, *dus-tifute*, referred primarily to an itinerant peddler, but could apply to any wayfarer found on English roads, especially a nonresident. This fifteenth-century compound word was borrowed from an earlier French term, either *pied-poudreux*, which meant "dusty-footed," or *pied puldreaux*, a peddler. *Piepowder courts* were established to temporarily sort out disputes between merchants and the public arising in the marketplace on fair days.

Its Latin forerunner was called the *pedis pulverizati*, "the court of the dusty foot." Theft and fraud, the most commonly tried crimes, were dealt with swiftly and harshly, since the local economies were heavily dependent on these markets. Blount's *Nomolexicon* ventured an explanation for the name, saying that these courts were "so called because they are most usual in summer, and suiters [plaintiffs and defendants] to this court are commonly country clowns with dusty feet." The last piepowder court was disbanded about 1850, although one located in Bristol endured well into the twentieth century. Butler provided this firsthand seventeenth-century account:

> Have its proceedings disallow'd, or
> Allow'd, at fancy of Pie-powder?
> Discover thieves, and bawds, recusants,
> Priests, witches, eves-droppers and nuisance:
> Tell who did play at games unlawful,
> And who fill'd pots of ale but half-full.

Williamson, in *Curious Survivals*, quoted an "ancient proclamation" issued in the town of Ely:

> All vagabonds, idle and misbehaving persons, all cheaters, cozeners, rogues, steady beggars and shifters do depart out of this fair immediately after this proclamation of the Bishop, upon pain of imprisonment and further correction by the [Piepowder] Court in the fair, that his majesty's good subjects may be the more quiet, and that the King's peace may be the better upheld.

In *Pilgrim's Progress*, John Bunyan wrote of this institution, calling it *Vanity Fair*, and the brutality associated with it. Those at fairs who transgressed the rules of the guilds, or were caught cheating, were taken to court, where a jury was quickly impaneled, evidence given, a sentence pronounced, and the perpetrators enstocked on a pillory, imprisoned, or even burned at the stake, all in the vicinity of the fair.

CUCKING-STOOL * An instrument of punishment, also known as a *scolding-stool*, in use from the thirteenth century until 1809. It was used for misdemeanor offenders, especially *scolds*, disorderly women whose loud derisive speech had become intolerable. A sign on a fourteenth-century cucking-stool in Canterbury warned, "Unfaithful wives beware, also butchers, bakers, brewers, apothecaries and all who give short measure." Borlase's 1754 *Natural History of Cornwall* rendered the following account of this device:

> Among the punishments inflicted in Cornwall of old time, was that of the cocking-stool, a seat of infamy where strumpets and scolds, with bare foot and head, were condemned the derision of those that passed by, for such time as the bailiffs of manors, which had the privilege of such jurisdictions did appoint.

The seventeenth-century *cockqueane-stool*, a specially made chair, allowed the condemned to be bound and exposed to the insults of the local citizenry. Chambers's *Book of Days* reported: "In

Scotland, an ale-wife who exhibited bad drink to the public was put upon the Cock stule, and the ale . . . was given to the poor." Depending on their transgression, detainees might also have been carried to a nearby body of water, such as a river or *ducking-pond*, for immersion. This excerpt from Benjamin West's 1780 *Ducking Stool* retains the flavor of this old method of reform:

There stands, my friend, in yonder pool
An engine call'd the Ducking-Stool:
By legal pow'r commanded down,
The joy and terror of the town.
If noisy dames should once begin,
To drive the house with horrid din,
Away you cry, you'll grace the stool,
We'll teach you how your tongue to rule.
Down in the deep the stool descends,
But here, at first, we miss our ends,
She mounts again, and rages more
Than ever vixen did before.
If so, my friend, pray let her take
A second turn into the lake;
No brawling wives, no furious wenches
No fire so hot but water quenches.

PETTY-FOGGER * Derogatory term used from the sixteenth to nineteenth centuries to indicate a "lip-wise" lawyer.
For a fee, these attorneys were willing to quibble over insig-
nificant legal points, jokingly dubbed *trickum legis*, or use unethical practices in order to win a case. Dyche wrote that these
legulians were "among the lawyers, what a quack is among physicians, one that rather increases suits than justly settles people's rights and properties." This was accomplished, Dyche
continued, by *petty-fogging*, that is, "setting people together by
the ears, and promoting quarrels, by assuring each party of
gaining advantage, by going to law upon trifling occasions."
Benjamin Franklin's opinion of these clever scoundrels was implied in *Poor Richard's Almanack:*

God works wonders, now and then;
Behold! A lawyer and an honest man.

Butler warned his readers about the consequences of dealing with attorneys:

> Others believe no voice t' an organ
> So sweet as lawyer's in his bar-gown,
> Until, with subtle cobweb-cheats,
> They're catch'd in knotted law, like nets;
> In which, when once they are imbrangled,
> The more they stir, the more they're tangled;
> And while their purses can dispute,
> There's no end of th' immortal suit.

Lewis Carroll ridiculed these *pettyfogulizing* counselors in *Alice in Wonderland:*

> "In my youth," said his father, "I took to the law,
> And argued each case with my wife;
> And the muscular strength, which it gave to my jaw,
> Has lasted the rest of my life."

Petty-fogger and its derivatives developed about the same time as *pettifactor*, a less derisive word for a legal agent who accepted simpler cases. Both these lawyers were, however, inclined to "walk the round," a phrase meaning to loiter around churches before, during, and after services, as a means of developing a clientele. One old account, in describing their strolling solicitations, said that they appeared to *squiny*, a sixteenth- to seventeenth-century verb defined by Joseph Shipley's *Dictionary of Early English* as "To look sidelong or invitingly, as a prostitute on the prowl."

USUFRUCT * Anglo-Norman legal term meaning literally "fruit usage." In practice, through the fifteenth century, usufruct allowed local residents to cross one another's property as long as the land was not harmed or altered. By the seventeenth century, according to Blount, *usufructry* came to signify "one that hath the use and reaps the profit of that, whereof the propriety doth rest in another." Roman law included the con-

cept of one person restoring the property of another after usage. One common example was cited by Harland:

> That the flock, often consisting of 2,000 sheep, or more, is the property of the lord, and delivered to the tenant by a schedule, subject to the condition of delivering up an equal number of the same quality at the expiration of the term. The practice . . . seems to have arisen from the difficulty of procuring tenants who were able to stock farms of such extent.

As implied by its literal meaning, early usufructry statutes also included the right to gather "windfall" fruit (that blown down by windstorms), or fallen pieces of firewood. Under the cover of usufructry, peasants sometimes used long-handled *bill-hooks* and shepherds' crooks to pull down fruit and branches that, they reasoned, would have come down eventually. But by the fourteenth century, this practice had been observed often enough to cause *crook* also to mean "to steal by deception," much as it does today. The clandestine use of a hooked staff, both rurally and in towns, to steal from otherwise inaccessible open windows led to the expression "by hook or by crook."

TREADMILL * Nineteenth-century piece of prison hardware (or architecture) contrived by William Cubitt to serve as a disciplinary tool, which occasionally performed useful work with its man-powered revolving horizontal shaft. In the 1820s, the English penal system introduced this form of punishment, intended to make prisoners wearily repent their crimes, the general design of which is still in use in modern gyms under brand names such as the StairMaster. By the late nineteenth century, the name of this machine was synonymous with monotony and exhaustion, as Sydney Smith wrote in 1824: "The

labour of the tread-mill is irksome, dull, monotonous and disgusting to the last degree." Hunter's *Encyclopædic Dictionary* outlined the treadmill's potential output: "The power may be utilized in grinding corn or turning machinery." But in actual application, London's *Daily News* of 1887 reported that this contraption and its counterpart, the *tread-wheel*, were of little use: "The authorities recently declared that they could buy flour cheaper than they could grind it." Hunter went on to remark that the treadmill was often "not revolved to any useful effect, a brake being simply attached to the axle." He suggested that the treadmill was decommissioned in part because of an unfair design flaw: "The weak and the strong are by it compelled to equal exertion." Prisoners put to work on the treadmill were often unprepared for its grueling workouts, or the pummeling they received from the guards if they bogged down, as the lines from a nineteenth-century song illustrate:

> Oh, stop the mill, stop the mill, stop it, I pray,
> For I have been treading a good deal today.
> My head is quite sore from the thumps I've received
> And my bones ache so much that sorely I'm grieved.

CATCHPOULE * Old English term for a "tax-gatherer" from the Latin *cacepollus*, literally "one who chases fowls." Catchpoule, which is unrelated to *cachpule* (see page 97), also signified the fourteenth-century sheriff's *bum-bailiff*, or petty officer (referred to as a *catch-rogue* in Norfolk), who originally *catchpoll'd* citizens, sometimes living up to his name by confiscating poultry for nonpayment of taxes. Later, the phonetically similar *catchpole* referred to an unusual eighteenth-century instrument that replaced the human touch, as Chambers described:

> The law-officer whose business was to apprehend criminals [including tax-evaders] . . . obtained that designation because he originally carried with him a pole fitted by a peculiar apparatus to catch a flying offender by the neck. The pole was about six feet in length, and the steel implement at its summit was sufficiently flexible to allow the neck to slip past the V-shaped arms and go into the collar, when the criminal was at the mercy of the officer to be pushed forward to prison or dragged behind him.

The catchpole was used to apprehend fleeing suspects, just as its modern counterpart is used by dogcatchers to collar wayward canines. In 1784, William Cowper wrote that a task could be accomplished "fast as catchpole claws can seize the slippery prey."

FIXFAX * Scottish word for a stocks-like neck-binding framework, derived from the fixfax ligaments, or "sinews in the necks of cattle or sheep," and from the German *flachs*, a sinew. The fixfax had a variety of forms, some of which featured holes cut to allow insertion of head and wrists of public offenders for display. How early this pillory was employed is not certain, but its use in publicly humiliating medieval citizens for misdeeds such as sales fraud, bad debts, and fortune-telling is known to have spread during the twelfth and thirteenth centuries. In the early 1800s, Charles Dickens, whose father spent time in debtor's prison, witnessed the pillory firsthand and characterized it—and other punishments—in *A Tale of Two Cities:*

> [an] institution that inflicted a punishment of which no one could foresee the extent . . . the whipping-post, another dear old institution, very humanising and softening to behold in action; also . . . blood-money, another fragment of ancestral wisdom, systematically leading to the most frightful mercenary crimes that could be committed under Heaven.

The fixfax was known by many dark-humored nicknames such as a *stretch-neck* in England, *Norway neckcloth*, if constructed of Norwegian fir, *thewe*, for women, who when enstocked were called "babes in the wood," *penance board*, for the religiously inclined, and *wooden parenthesis* for intellectuals. It was usually placed in a town square, where passersby would jeer at and pelt the confined with dangerous or humiliating projectiles including rotten vegetables, dead animals, spittle, and excrement. Leg stocks were prescribed for punishing the crimes of laziness

and vagrancy, offering locals a chance to tickle the feet of the incarcerated. In the sixteenth century, playwright Ben Jonson described someone going to a pillory, or *berlina:*

> Wearing a cap, with fair long ass's ears
> Instead of horns; and so to mount, a paper
> Pinn'd on thy breast, to the berlina.

Robinson Crusoe's author, Daniel Defoe, was once pilloried for his outspoken and unpopular political views. He won over the crowd, however, by distributing a lampoon he had written in 1703 about this bizarre punishment, called *A Hymn to the Pillory*, and was pelted with flowers instead of the usual abuse. The pillory was not completely abolished in England and America until 1837 and 1905 respectively.

———

ORDAL * Anglo-Saxon legal term for "the judgment of God," which was later called "trial by ordeal." This legal proceeding was administered in various ways, depending on the defendant's social status. Some were tested by immersion of their hands in hot water, followed by a check for blisters. If they appeared, their testimony was considered flawed. The

modern expression "being in hot water" stems from this practice. Suspected witches were subjected to an ordal known as "swimming the witch," since the holy medium of water was used in baptismal rites. Water would reject a real witch, it was believed, causing her to float, as set forth by Henry Bohn in a 1859 footnote to *Hudibras:*

> The common test for witchcraft was to throw the suspected witch into the water. If she swam, she was judged guilty; if she sank, she preserved her character and lost only her life. King James, in his *Daemonology*, explained the floating of the witch by the refusal of the element used in baptism to receive into its bosom one who had renounced the blessing of it. The last witch swum in England was an old woman in a village of Suffolk, about thirty years ago.

A private method of locating and eliminating the source of witchcraft was presented in Grose's *Provincial Glossary:*

> Some hair, the pairings of nails and urine of any person bewitched . . . being put into a stone bottle with crooked nails, corked close and tied down with wire, and hung up the chimney will cause the witch to suffer the most acute torments imaginable, til the bottle is uncorked, and the mixture dispursed; insomuch that they will even risk a detection by coming to the house and attempting to pull down the bottle.

The same procedure was faithfully employed and recorded by Joseph Glanvill in his 1688 *Palpable Evidence of Spirits and Witchcraft*, with these results:

> His wife began to mend . . . and in a competent time was finely well recovered. But there came a woman from a town some miles off to their house with a lamentable outcry, that they had killed her husband; that . . . husband was a wizard and had bewitched this man's wife.

Reginald Scot's 1584 *Discovery of Witchcraft* grimly summarized the justice imparted with these methods: "If you read the executions done upon witches, you shall see such impossibilities confessed as none, having his right wits, will believe."

NECKE-VERSE * Since as early as the eleventh century, if a prisoner convicted of a capital offense could read the first verse of the Fifty-first Psalm, he would often be pardoned. The catch was, however, that this "test" had to be undertaken in Latin, a language that few outside the Church could understand. If the condemned could not read the necke-verse, it was said that he must "sing it at the gallows," prompting these lines in *Hudibras:*

> And if they cannot read one verse
> I' th' Psalms, must sing it, and that's worse.

Throughout the Middle Ages and beyond, misdeeds of the clergy were punished by divine authority, it was assumed, and generally overlooked, or prosecuted with undue leniency by the Church. This unfair "loophole" in the law eventually evoked well-founded satirical criticism, such as this lampoon from the eighteenth-century periodical *British Apollo:*

> When Popery long since, with tenets of nonsense,
> And ignorance fill'd the land,
> And Latin alone to Church-men was known,
> And reading a legible hand.
> This privilege then, to save learned men,
> Was granted 'em by Holy Church,
> While villains whose crimes, were lesser nine times,
> Were certainly left in the lurch.
> If a monk had been taken, for stealing of bacon,
> For burglary, murder or rape;
> If he could but rehearse, [well prompt] his Neck Verse,
> He never could fail to escape.

This controversial exemption from criminal prosecution was ironically known as "benefit of clergy," a phrase that has since been altered to mean a prisoner's access to a priest. Even the illegitimate children of monks, and in some cases church janitors and workmen, were often shielded by Church laws until the 1600s.

———

HIDEGILD * Anglo-Saxon word in which *hide*, skin, and *gild*, money, combined to denote "a fine paid in lieu of a flogging" for various kinds of misconduct. Or, for one lucky enough to have been born a prince, and not subject to physical punishment, a servant, sometimes called a "whipping-boy," endured for royalty a *chaw-buck*, a seventeenth-century word for a flogging. The two boys' relationship is illustrated in *Hudibras:*

And that is, if a man may do't
By proxy whipp'd, or substitute . . .
Justice gives sentence, many times,
On one man for another's crimes.

Herrick also alluded to this practice in his *Hesperides:*

Good princes must be prayed for: For the bad
They must be borne with, and in rev'rence had.
Do they first pill [plunder] thee, next, pluck off thy skin?
Good children kisse [feel] the rods that punish sin.

It was reasoned that the prince, who was required to watch, would experience his friend's discomfort and absorb the pain

vicariously. Historians believe, however, that these "lessons," more often than not, instilled in the prince an arrogant sense of the power and privilege of rank.

AMBODEXTER * A contemptuous term for an unethical lawyer, or sometimes a "juror," who received fees from a defendant as well as a plaintiff in the same case, from the fifteenth to eighteenth centuries. Ambodexter could also apply to a "double-dealing" witness, known sometimes as a *post-knight*, because of his habit of loitering near the posts on which the sheriff's

proclamations were affixed. The post-knight would swear to a false testimony in exchange for money, as mentioned in Butler's *Hudibras:*

> Like knights o' the post, and falsely charge
> Upon themselves what others forge;
> As if they were consenting to
> All mischief in the world men do.

The Latin prefix *amb*, "both," is found in another archaic term associated with legal verbiage, *ambiloquent*, which at that time meant "competent with double-talk." To give themselves more work, lawyers often urged their clients to continue lawsuits when the latter were ready to seek settlement, or to file spurious claims. Butler continued:

> So lawyers, lest the bear defendant,
> And plaintiff dog, should make an end on't,
> Do stave and tail with writs of error,
> Reverse of judgment and demurrer,
> To let them breathe awhile, and then
> Cry whoop, and set them on again.

In Norfolk and Suffolk, attorneys were also accused of being "cow-tongued," that is, of having a tongue like a cow's, figuratively smooth on one side and rough on the other. Benjamin Franklin alluded to this:

> I know you lawyers can, with ease,
> Twist words and meanings as you please;
> That language, by your skill made pliant,
> Will bend to favour every client;
> That 'tis the fee directs the sense
> To make out either side's pretence;
> When you peruse the clearest case,
> You see it with a double face,
> For skepticism's your profession;
> You hold there's doubt in all expression.

It was perhaps with the ambodexter in mind that sixteenth-century religious reformer Martin Luther wrote, "My greatest wish is that none of my children become lawyers."

5. Occupational Hazards
Rattoners, Eye-Servants, and Mop-Fairs

BARBI-TONSORIBUS * One who shaved or otherwise cut hair professionally, borrowed directly from Latin about 1300. Before the year 1000, barbers visited monasteries to cut the monks' *tonsures* as dictated by their religious order. There, the barbers acted as surgical assistants, learning the art of *chirurgery* (literally "hand work," or surgery), while creating in their wake the basis for the seventeenth-century proverb "Barbers first learn to shave by shaving fools." These "tonsors," as they were called, were frequent targets for satire, as in these lines from William Combe's *Dr. Syntax* trilogy:

> Go with the tonsor, Pat, and try
> To aid his hand and guide his eye.

They began performing such procedures as tooth extraction and scaling, abscess lancing, bloodletting, removal of urinary stones, and many others, as noted in a historical sketch from Timbs's 1855 *Curiosities of London:*

> In 1512, an Act was passed to prevent any besides barbers practising surgery within the City and seven miles round. . . . In 1540 they [barbers and surgeons] were united into one corporate body. . . . The Barber-Surgeons are exempt, as formerly, from serving as constables or on the nightly watch, on juries, inquests attaints or recognisances. After the separation of the two professions, the barbers continued to let blood (whence the pole) and draw teeth until our time. The last we remember of this class, and with

pain, was one Middleditch, in Southwark, in whose window were displayed heaps of drawn teeth.

A patient's discomfort might have been minimized by a procedure found in Culpeper's *Herbal*—if the barber could read: "To draw a tooth without pain, fill an earthen crucible full of emmets, ants or pismires, eggs and all, and when you have burned them, keep the ashes, with which if you touch a tooth it will fall out." John Gay, in his 1727 *Fable of the Goat Without a Beard*, visited a "tonsorial parlor":

> His pole with pewter basons hung,
> Black rotten teeth in order strung,
> Did well his threefold trade explain,
> Who shav'd, drew teeth and breathed a vein.

Despite the legislation of 1512, medical licensing over the next four centuries continued to be poorly administered and infractions dealt with leniently. As late as 1863 the work of a London barrister stated:

> Any person who shall falsely pretend to be registered, or take or use the name or title of a physician, surgeon, general practitioner or apothecary, will be liable, on a summary conviction, to a fine of £20.

In his 1813 *Popular Antiquities*, Brand wrote of the "gross ignorance" of barbers, who seem to have preferred "hands-on" experience to learning terminology. Brand cited an extract from *Wonders of the World* in which a barber, after cupping and bleeding the book's author, asks him if he would be "sacrificed":

> Sacrificed, said I? Did the physician tell you any such thing? No (quoth he) but I have sacrificed many who have been the better for it. Then, musing a little with myself, I told him, surely . . . you mean "scarified." O, sir, by

your favour, (quoth he) I have ever heard it called sacrificing, and as for scarifying, I have never heard of it before.
. . . Since which time I never saw any man in a barber's
hands but that sacrificing barber came to my mind.

The red-and-white-striped English barber pole originated from
the barber-surgeon's practice of wrapping rinsed out bandages
around a red pole to dry. At the base of the pole is usually
seen a metallic cap that represents the bowl once used to catch
blood. The blue stripe was added later, mainly in America.

BILLINGSGATRY * The superlatively vigorous and explicitly blunt language made famous at Billingsgate, one of two
gates that controlled access to London via the Thames. This
originally Roman construction became a marketplace for various commodities, especially grain, and remained as such until
the end of the seventeenth century. At that time, it was designated as a site for selling seafood only, and developed a reputation for unrestrained verbal doggery, particularly by women.
In *London Labour and the London Poor*, Henry Mayhew recorded
observations of this place, along with some of the more civil
calls he heard there in the 1850s:

The morning air is filled with a kind of seaweedy odour,
reminding one of the sea-shore; and on entering the market, the smell of fish . . . is almost overpowering. . . .
Over the hum of the voices is heard the shouts of the
salesmen who, with their white aprons, peering above
the heads of the mob, stand on their tables roaring out
the prices. All are bawling together—salesmen and hucksters of provisions, capes, hardware and newspapers—till
the place is a perfect Babel of competition. "Ha-a-ansom
cod! Best in the market! All alive! alive! alive-Oh! . . . Ye-
o-o! Here's your fine Yarmouth bloaters! Who's the

buyer? . . . Here's food for your belly and clothes for your back, but I sell food for the mind (shouts the newsvendor). . . . Had-had-haddock! All fresh and good!"

Buttwife, a Middle English word for a boundless-tongued fisherman's wife, or "fishwife," signified one who sold flatfish and created what were once referred to as vocal "ear-sores" in her vicinity. Raphael Holinshed, in his 1577 *Chronicles of England, Scotland and Ireland*, referred to a particularly offensive manner of speaking: "as bad a tongue . . . as any oyster-wife at Billings-

gate." The catch that this colorfully argumentative fishmongress peddled often included turbot, flounder, skate, and the prized "haly butt" (halibut), once eaten almost exclusively on Church-dictated meat-fasting days. Such days once numbered almost one hundred eighty per year.

———

FLUNKEY ❋ Eighteenth-century term for a footman or "servant in livery." It was derived from the French verb *flanquer*, which meant, according to etymologist Walter Skeat, "To flanke, run along by the side of . . . to be at one's elbow for a help at need." Jamieson believed flunkey to have hailed from an old Swedish expression "en flink gaasse," "a brisk lad, one fit to serve with alertness." As late as the 1830s and 1840s, flunkey developed its modern pejorative meaning from college slang for an academic failure or one who slavishly obeyed another. The flunkey's older cousin, the *lackey*, had a similarly innocent inception as a sixteenth-century foot soldier or bowman. Lackey, which was spelled more than a dozen known ways, was also used to indicate a footman, before acquiring its disrespectful overtones. In *The Taming of the Shrew*, Biondello, himself a servant, used this term without malice: "O sir! his lackey, for all the world comparisoned . . . not like a Christian footboy or a gentleman's lackey."

Through the early 1780s, the *running-footman*, another

name for the flunkey, was a servant who tended horse-drawn carriages, often trotting ahead or alongside for distances of up to twenty miles. His duties included lighting the way with torches, paying tolls, keeping carriage wheels and horses from bogging down in potholes on the unreliable roads, and dealing with innkeepers regarding the arrival of his master's party. Some of these footmen carried special batons, ostensibly to prod the horses or defend themselves, but having one end that unscrewed to allow access to liquor, wine and egg whites being a favorite. In 1657, William Coles's *Adam in Eden* presented an herb highly esteemed by travelers and lackeys alike:

> The decoction of the herb Lady's Bedstraw, being yet warm, is of admirable use to bathe the feet of travellers; and for lackeys . . . whose long running causeth not only weariness but stiffness . . . to both of which this herb is so friendly, that it makes them to become so lissom, as if they had never been abroad.

One of eighteenth-century England's best-known authorities on liquor and nightlife, Samuel Johnson, wrote: "There is nothing which has yet been contrived by man, by which so much happiness is produced as by a good tavern or inn."

———————

BIRD-SWINDLER * Nineteenth-century expression for a fraudulent purveyor of expensive, exotic-looking birds that, upon closer inspection, were found to be one of several common varieties of local birds that had been trimmed and dyed. The green finch was commonly used, since its light-colored plumage was easily adapted for such purposes. These birds were caught, often at night, in a manner reminiscent of the old French proverb, "One man beats the bush and another catches the bird," according to Markham's 1621 *Hunger's Prevention:*

> The air being mild and the moon not shining, you shall take your low-bell [and] . . . a net at least twenty yards deep . . . go into some stubble field, and he which carrieth the bell shall go foremost and toll the bell as he goeth along solemnly. Then having spread your net where you think any game is, you shall light bundles of dry straw that will blaze. . . . For the use of these instruments is that the sound of the bell makes the birds to lie close whilst you are pitching your net . . . then the suddenness

of the light blazing makes them to spring up, while the net stays and entangles them.

Daniel Pell offered some questionable bird lore in his 1659 *Improvement of the Sea:* "The dodderil, of whom they say that whatsoever is done in the sight of her, she will exactly imitate." Francis Willughby's 1672 *Ornithologia*, however, confirmed Pell's odd tale, and offered an imaginative method of ensnarement:

> The dotterel is a very foolish bird . . . taken in the night by the light of candle; for if he [a bird-catcher] stretches out an arm, that also stretches out a wing; if a foot, that likewise a foot; in brief, whatever the fowler doth, the same doth the bird; and so being intent upon men's gestures, it is deceived and covered with the net spread for it.

Mayhew presented a statistical portrait of a London bird-catcher with an amazing record, even allowing for exaggeration:

> For almost sixty years, almost without intermission, Old Gilham caught birds. I am assured that to state that his catch during this long period averaged a hundred a week, hens included, is within the mark, for he was a most indefatigable man; even at that computation, however, he would have been the captor, in his lifetime, of three hundred and twelve thousand birds!

A strong market for local birds existed because the availability of canaries from the Spanish Canary Islands was carefully controlled by the Spanish Church in Elizabethan times, and only the export of male birds was allowed.

RATTONER * Professional fourteenth-century forerunner of the exterminator, known commonly as the *rat-catcher*, and until the 1850s, the *rat-charmer*. The term rattoner was inspired by the Old French *raton* and Medieval Latin *ratonis*, both words for the pesky rodent. Mayhew, in interviewing one worker,

discovered that there was surprisingly little utilization of rattoners by grain warehouse owners:

> One great source of the rat-catcher's employment . . . thirty years ago, or even to a later period, is now comparatively a nonentity. At that time the rat-catcher received a yearly or quarterly stipend to keep a London granary clear of rats. I was told by a man who has for twenty-eight years been employed about London granaries, that he had never known a rat-catcher employed in one except about twenty or twenty-two years ago, and that was in a granary by the river-side. . . . That same man told me that he had been, five or six times, applied to by rat-catchers, and with liberal offers of beer, to allow them to try and capture the black rats of the granary.

It was formerly believed that rodents could be removed from a dwelling by reciting or posting poetry, as found in Ben Jonson's *Poetaster:* "Rhime them to death, as they do Irish rats." Chambers's 1826 *Popular Rhymes of Scotland* offered a dignified method of "eviction":

When these creatures become superabundant in a house of the humbler class, a writ of ejectment . . . is served upon them by being stuck up legibly written on the wall:

Ratton and mouse,
Lea' the puir woman's house;
Gang awa' owre by to 'e mill,
And there . . . 'a ye'll get your fill.

By the 1850s, dogs such as terriers, known as *ratters*, had become so popular for their rodent-ridding abilities that a tax was levied upon them in England.

———————

EYE-SERVANT * Defamatory expression for a devious domestic or other employee, also called an *eye-waiter* from the 1500s to the 1830s, who was too lazy to efficiently perform duties except when "within eyeshot" of his or her master—a form of insincerity known as "eye-service." One medieval explanation for this phenomenon was that servants were stricken with *idle worms*, tiny worms believed to grow and multiply on their fingers when they were not busy. These wriggly creatures were alluded to in *Romeo and Juliet*, when Mercutio spoke of "a round little worm, pricked from the lazy finger of a maid." About that time, to be "sick of the idles" also referred to the condition of laziness, according to *Withal's Dictionary* of 1634. In this regard, Isaac Watts wrote in his 1715 *Songs for Children*,

In works of labour or of skill,
I would be lazy too,
For Satan finds some mischief still
For idle hands to do.

The term *fever-lurden* once related to a "medical condition" common in servants now known as laziness, according to an account of 1547, "with which yonge persons bee sore infected nowe a dayes." Turner's *Herbal* contains a remedy for lazy servants: "Mustard is also good to be laid upon the heads of them that have the Drowsy Evil or forgetful sickness called Lethargies; after that the hair is shaven off." Jonathan Swift, in *Directions to Servants*, offered the following practical advice to eye-servants:

> If your master or lady happen to accuse you wrongfully, you are a happy servant, for you have nothing more to do than, for every [subsequent] fault you commit while you are in their service, to put them in mind of that false accusation, and protest yourself equally innocent. . . . When you are chidden for a fault, as you go out of the room and down the stairs, mutter loud enough to be plainly heard; this will make him believe you are innocent.

EGGLER * An egg dealer of the 1700s, whose business, *eggling*, consisted of collecting the produce of *egg-beds* (a Scottish term for "the ovaries of a fowl"), as well as the financial operations. Mayhew gave an account of an eggler:

> The young gypsy-looking lad . . . was peculiarly picturesque in appearance. He wore a dirty-looking smock-frock with large pockets at the side; he had no shirt, and his long black hair hung in curls about him, contrasting strongly with his bare white neck and chest. The broad-brimmed brown Italian-looking hat, broken in and ragged at the top, threw a dark half-mask-like shadow over the upper part of his face. His feet were bare and black with mud; he carried in one hand his basket of nests, dotted with their many coloured eggs; in the other hand he held

a live snake that writhed and twisted as its metallic-looking skin glistened in the sun.

Unusual by-products he offered along with eggs were whatever complete birds' nests could be found, as we hear in the boy's monologue:

> There's one gentleman as I sells to is a wholesale dealer in window glass—and he has a hobby for them. He puts 'em into glass cases and makes presents of 'em to his friends. . . . I've sold him a hundred nesties, I'm sure. I sells a nest now and then to a lady with a child, but the boys of twelve to fifteen years of age is my best friends. They buy 'em only for curiosity. I sold three partridge eggs yesterday to a gentleman, and he would put them under a bantam he'd got, and hatch 'em.

Saint Simon of Cyrene, an eggler by trade, was a bystander as Jesus carried the cross bound for Calvary. A theory promoted by a medieval Gnostic sect suggested that Simon not only carried the cross but, by somehow exchanging bodies, endured the crucifixion. When he later "returned" to his own body, he found that his eggs had been fantastically decorated, a story that led to the coloring tradition. Eggs, which have long symbolized rebirth, became associated with Easter in another way. During the forty days of Lent preceding this holiday, eggs were forbidden by the Church and generally not eaten. Hens continued to lay and after six weeks a surplus had often accumulated, which needed to be consumed quickly.

MOP-FAIR   *   From the 1600s until the twentieth century, annual opportunity for employers in English and Welsh districts to find domestic and agricultural workers. At these events, which were known locally as *mapps* and sometimes held on Saint Martin's Day, unmarried servants—often numbering in the hundreds—stood in lines wearing occupational emblems.

Grooms carried a piece of sponge, while household domestics carried a mop, from which this assembly borrowed its name. Eden described some mop-fair participants in his 1797 work, *State of the Poor:*

> Each person has a badge or external mark, expressive of his occupation. A carter exhibits a piece of whip-cord tied to his hat; a cowherd has a lock of cow-hair in his; and the dairy-maid has the same descriptive mark attached to

her breast. Even in London, brick-layers and other house-labourers carry their representative implements to the places where they stand for hire.

In his seventeenth century *History of Oxfordshire*, Robert Plot added that "the shepherds [stood] with their crooks . . . but the maids . . . stood promiscuously." Earnest money, called *God's-penny* in northern England, or more generally the "fastening-penny," ranged from a shilling to a pound and was given to the contracted worker, as this excerpt from London's *Daily Mail*, written a few days after a mop-fair of 1903, attested:

> As soon as a bargain is struck, the hired men and maidens display knots of bright coloured ribbons, and the rest of the day is spent among the swings and roundabouts. The present year's experience betrayed a decline in the interest shown and in the attendance.

Elaborate food often enticed workers to these events, as shown by a 1912 article from the *Daily Sketch:*

> The Stratford-on-Avon Mop Fair, which dates from the reign of King John, was held on Saturday. Six excursion trains ran from London, and specials arrived from many towns. The ox-roasting in the streets was one of the principal sights of the Fair, seven bullocks and a dozen pigs being spitted.

A "runaway mop" was the same sort of fair held a few weeks after the customary ones, featuring the servants who had been hired earlier but had, for whatever reason, run away from their previous situations.

———

TOSHER * Name given to eighteenth- to nineteenth-century "sewer-hunters," based upon their own term, *tosh*, which referred to the articles—especially those made of copper—painstakingly gathered along the Thames. These scavengers were presented in unembellished detail by Mayhew as

> . . . habited in long greasy velveteen coats, furnished with pockets of vast capacity, and their nether limbs encased in dirty canvas trousers, and any old slops of shoes, that may be fit only for wading through the mud. They carry a bag on their back, and in their hand a pole seven or eight feet long, on one end of which is a large iron hoe . . . with it they try the ground wherever it appears unsafe, before venturing on it, and, assured of its safety, walk forward steadying their footsteps with the staff. Although they cannot "pick up" as much now as they formerly did . . . they can afford to look down with a species of aristocratic contempt on the puny efforts of their less fortunate bretheren, the "mud-larks" [children who scavenged in muddy river beds].

Mayhew also suggested that toshers earned a better living than many of their comparably uneducated peers, including artisans and clerks, but managed their money poorly:

There were known to be a few years ago nearly 200 . . . toshers, and, incredible as it may appear, I have satisfied myself that, taking one week with another, they could not be said to make much short of £2 per week. . . . The sewer-hunters, strange as it may appear, are certainly smart fellows, and take decided precedence of all the other "finders" of London . . . on account of . . . the skill and courage they manifest in the pursuit of their dangerous employment. But, like all who make a living, as it were, by a game of chance . . . they no sooner make a "haul," as they say, than they adjourn to some low public-house in the neighborhood, and seldom leave till empty pockets and hungry stomachs drive them forth to procure the means for a fresh debauch.

Smyth's 1867 *Sailor's Word-book* implied that the tosher had a more destructive and malevolent occupation, being "one who, on the Thames, steals copper from ship's bottoms."

6. The Confusion of Tongues
Bibliomaniacs, Goliards, and Dunsmen

BIBLIOMANIAC * Someone with a lunatic's passion for acquiring books, as this word's roots imply. Chambers portrayed England's most famous bibliomaniac, Richard Heber (1773–1833) as an obsessive collector:

> The bibliomaniac collects books merely for the pleasure of collecting. . . . On hearing of a curious book, he was known to have put himself into a mail coach and travelled three or four hundred miles to obtain it, fearful to entrust his commission to anyone else.

Heber's family inheritance allowed him to indulge his desire for literary acquisition, and spend immense sums to purchase books, which he did personally through local booksellers called *bibliopolists*, and through correspondence throughout the British Isles, France, and the Low Countries. After building an unparalleled collection on subjects such as Old English literature, he branched into Latin, Greek, French, Italian, and even Portuguese. When asked about his habit of collecting multiple copies of the same works, he replied, according to his biographer,

> Why you see, sir, no man can do comfortably without three copies of a work. One he must have for a show-copy, and he will probably keep it at his country-house. Another he will require for his own use and reference; and unless he is inclined to part with this, which is very inconvenient, or risk the injury of his best copy, he must needs have a third at the service of his friends.

Chambers gave an overview of Heber's "libraries":

> His house at Hodnet, in Shropshire, was nearly all library. His house in Pimlico, where he died in 1833, was filled with books from top to bottom, every chair, table and passage containing "piles of erudition." A house in York Street, Westminster, was similarly filled. He had immense collections of books in houses rented merely to contain them at Oxford, Paris, Antwerp, Brussels and Ghent.

Amazingly, when Heber died his will did not even acknowledge his books. His *bibliolatry* had driven him to acquire, by one

estimate, half a million books, but in their disposal after his death they were treated simply as so much property in the hands of an auctioneer. Sotheby's sale of a portion of the books required two hundred and two working days spanning more than two years. It was reckoned that the proceeds of his books amounted to only about two thirds of the books' original cost.

In *A Tale of a Tub*, Jonathan Swift advised readers without much education or literary interest how to appear scholarly:

> The most accomplished way of using books at present is two-fold: either, first, to serve them as some men do

lords, learn their titles exactly, and then brag of their acquaintance. Or, secondly . . . to get a thorough insight into the index, by which the whole book is governed and turned, like fishes by the tail.

MUMPSIMUS * Middle English noun denoting an incorrigible, dogmatic old pedant—jokingly called a *foolosopher* about 1550—which grew to mean any incorrect opinion stubbornly clung to. Mumpsimus was taken from the Latin *sumpsimus*, a word which was incorrectly copied and read for years in mass by a *lack-Latin*, an illiterate fifteenth-century English preacher.

Upon being shown his error, this obstinate clergyman reportedly replied, "I will not change my old mumpsimus for your new sumpsimus." This attitude was often ridiculed by French writer Michel Montaigne, who elegantly wrote of a common human blind spot, "I never met a man who thought his thinking was faulty." Songs that mocked theological arrogance, such as this anonymous eighteenth-century lampoon *The Deist*, became very popular:

Religion's a political law,
Devised by the prigs of the schools,

To keep the rabble in awe,
And amuse poor bigoted fools.
And they for good victuals and bub [drink]
Will bellow their nonsense aloud
And cant out a tale of a tub
To frighten the poor ignorant crowd.
Though the apple was but a fib,
Yet he vouches it to be true;
And that Eve was made of a rib,
Pray, gentlemen, what think you?
I pity the flogging old shaver,
Who pretends he does miracles show,
And makes flesh and blood of a wafer
A baker has just made the dough.

A lawyer with the narrow-mindedness of a mumpsimus was sometimes called a *jurisprude*.

CHAMBERDEACON * Term of obscure origin, probably derived from the Medieval Latin phrase *in camera degentes*, "living in a chamber." Chamberdeacon described an impoverished fifteenth-century Irish scholar, or one preparing to take "minor orders" (such as would be necessary for a minister's assistant), who haunted English universities, particularly Oxford, without actually belonging to a college or residence hall. Sometimes called "bedders," they supported themselves by performing domestic services for well-to-do scholars, and reputedly augmented their incomes in less honest ways. In 1749, for example, Bailey presented these shadowy figures as thieves: "Irish beggars, in the habits of poor scholars of Oxford, who oft committed robberies." In 1432, Anthony à Woods questioned their academic intentions in a dark, contemporary portrayal of them as

> Irish beggars who . . . would often disturb the peace of
> the university, live under no government of principles

... and in the night-time go abroad to commit spoils and manslaughter, lurk about in taverns and houses of ill-report, commit burglaries and such like.

Williamson's *Curious Survivals* offered the derivation of a modern slang word, based on the chamberdeacon's lifestyle:

A popular word in the streets is "cad," and this we take from a dead body, "cadaver." Originally, persons called cads were those living in a University, but were not members of that university. The graduates were divided into "men," and those who were not men of the college, and thence grew up a habit of speaking of those who were not members as dead.

Eventually, there were "decisive measures taken in Oxford against the *Chamberdekyns*," according to an 1831 account by Sir William Hamilton.

GOLIARD ✳ An Old French expression originally denoting a glutton, whose meaning was broadened in *Piers Plowman* (1377) to a "glouten of wordes." Skeat said of these men, whom he called *goliardeys:*

This jovial sect seems to have been so called from Golias, the real or assumed name of a man of wit, towards the end of the thirteenth century. . . . Soon after, Goliardus meant a clerical buffoon; still later, it meant any jongleur, or any teller of ribald stories, in which sense it was used by Chaucer.

These itinerant scholar-jesters of the twelfth and thirteenth centuries specialized in *goliardery*, the composition and recital of satirical *latinities* or Latin verse. Latin was certainly not popular with everyone at that time, as a line from Shakespeare's

Henry IV illustrates: "Away with him! Away with him! He speaks Latin." And again, in *Love's Labour's Lost*, Shakespeare exposed the trickery employed by doctors, lawyers, and the Church: "O, I smell false Latin."

Montaigne had a mixed opinion of learning Latin: "I must needs acknowledge that the Greek and Latin tongues are great ornaments in a gentleman, but they are purchased at an over-high rate." Knowledge of classical languages had other benefits, as Jamieson pointed out in referring to an 1818 edition of *Rob Roy:* "He understood Greek, Latin and Hebrew, and therefore . . . needed not to care for ghost, devil or dobbie." Butler described a sixteenth-century goliard's speech:

> It was a parti-coloured dress
> Of patch'd and piebald [interwoven] languages;
> 'Twas English cut on Greek and Latin,
> Like fustian heretofore on satin.
> It had an old promiscuous tone
> As if h' had talk'd three parts in one;
> Which made some think, when he did gabble,
> Th' had heard three labourers of Babel.

The *jarkman* (from *jark*, a "certification"), a sixteenth-century descendant of the goliard, was a vagabond who used his literary talents underhandedly. In his 1561 work, *The Fraternitye of Vagabondes*, John Awdelay describes the jarkman as "he that can write and reade, and sometime speake latin. He useth [these skills] to make counterfaite licences which they call gybes, and sets to seales, in their language [falsified documents] called jarks." Mayhew recounted a story about a latter-day practitioner of the goliard and jarkman's trade, known as a "lurker":

> These professional writers are in possession of many autographs of charitable persons, and as they keep a dozen or more bottles of ink, and seldom write two documents on the same sort of paper, it is difficult to detect the

imposition. A famous lurker . . . was once taken before a magistrate at York whose own signature was attached to his fakement. The imitation was excellent, and the lurker swore hard and fast to the worthy justice that he (the justice) did write it in his saddle-room. . . . The effrontery and firmness of the prisoner's statement gained him his discharge.

FERULE * Flat-edged wooden switch or stick, used by fifteenth- and sixteenth-century schoolteachers to physically discipline students. This feared instrument, known in the

eighteenth century as a "tickle tail," was made from the dried stem of a plant of the fennel family called the *ferula*, which grows abundantly in southern Europe. The London version of the ferule, the birch rod, was often itemized as a charge on eighteenth- and nineteenth-century children's school bills. Stephen Gosson's 1579 *Schoole of Abuse* related stories of the dreaded ferule: "I shoulde tel tales of the schoole, and bee feruled for my faults or hyssed at for a blab, yf I layde the orders open before your eyes." Schoolmasters were formerly called *bumbrushes*, another reference to their frequent use of corporal punishment administered to their pupils' posteriors, although a *pandy*, a blow to the palm of the hand with a ferule, was also common. Samuel Johnson once observed that "There is less flogging in our great schools than formerly—but then less is learned there; so that what the boys get at one end, they lose at the other."

For centuries, teachers also got away with charging their students for unusual extracurricular activities such as cockfighting, according to Brand's 1813 *Popular Antiquities* on the meaning of *cock-penny:* "The scholars of Clitheroe Free Grammar-School have to pay at Shrovetide what is called a cock-penny . . . supposed to be a substitute for bringing the animal itself to school, which formerly was very common."

In his seventeenth-century work, *The Grammar School*, Henry Peacham recalled one of his own instructors with an odd philosophy about education:

> I had, I remember, myself a master who by no entreaty would teach no scholar he had, further than his father had learned before him; if the father had only learnt but to read English, the son should go no further. His reason was that they would otherwise prove saucy rogues and rule their fathers.

In his *Journal*, former schoolteacher and staunch anti-ferulist Henry David Thoreau pronounced his opinion of contemporary education: "What does education do? It makes a straight-cut ditch of a free, meandering brook."

INKHORNISM * A literary composition of the sixteenth and seventeenth centuries that "smelled of the lamp," meaning it was overworked and unnecessarily intellectual, or *inkhornish*, perhaps from too much burning of midnight oil. A debate was stirred during the latter 1500s about whether to keep English "pure" by rejecting the inclusion of "Latinisms" and other foreign "inkhornism terms" not used in general conversation. *Inkhornism* was fathered in the 1590s by the name of a small portable case of writing instruments, called an *enkhorn* in the fourteenth to eighteenth centuries, which was usually made of horn but occasionally of wood or metal. It was mentioned in Shakespeare's *Henry IV*, when it was said of a character: "Hang him with his pen and ink-horn about his neck." These tools were typically carried by *pedagogues* (literally "boy leaders"), later used to indicate a pompous or pedantic schoolmaster. In his 1601 *Passions of the Minde*, Thomas Wright criticized those who relied on artificial language in their writing: "To use many metaphors in prose, or incke-pot terms, smelleth of affectation."

An eighteenth-century recipe found in *The Compleat House-wife* highlighted some of the strange ingredients and procedures involved in making ink:

> Get one pound of best galls, half a pound of copperas [copper sulfate], a quarter of a pound of gum arabick, a quarter of a pound of white sugar-candy; bruise the galls and beat your other ingredients fine, and infuse them all in three quarts of white wine or rain-water, and let them stand hot by the fire three or four days; then put all into a new pipkin; set it on a slow fire, so as not to boil; keep it frequently stirring, and let it stand five or six hours, till one quarter is consumed. And when cold, strain it through a clean coarse piece of linen; bottle it and keep it for use.

An *inkling*, the diminutive of ink, once indicated a sample or glimpse of a written idea, and was related to an older Anglo-Saxon verb *imt*, to mutter. *Inkshed*, used in the same sense as bloodshed, was unnecessary verbiage written or "spilled" by an *inkster*, an inferior writer.

BOWDLERIZE * To censor or purge a literary work by editorial omission of indelicate or potentially offensive passages, from the early 1830s. This word and a corresponding noun, *bowdlerism*, were inspired by a popular pre-Victorian edition of Shakespeare's "incomplete" works—stripped of overtones of and references to drinking, carousing, and general evil-doing—published in 1818 by the Reverend Thomas Bowdler for use as "family reading." In the preface, the author defends his sanitized version as one "in which those words and expressions are

omitted which cannot with propriety be read aloud in a family." Bowdler, a Scottish doctor who had abandoned a medical career thirty years earlier because his patients made him "queasy," explained that he wished to present this material without "anything that could raise a blush on the cheek of modesty." Bowdlerize, along with terms like *bowdlerization*, were used especially in satire and literary criticism into the early twentieth century. In 1886, Thomas Huxley opined regarding censorship: "We may fairly inquire whether editorial Bowdlerising has not prevailed over historic truth."

GRAMARYE * Medieval Scottish variation of Old French *gramaire*, meaning the study and application of any sort of "book-learning," or *grammar*. Jamieson suggested that literary skills were regarded with suspicion in medieval times as magic or the devil's work: "In those dark and ignorant ages, when it was thought a high degree of learning to be able to read and write, he who made a little further progress in literature might well pass for a conjurer or magician." This belief was reflected by another borrowed French word, *grimoire*, a book of magic spells. We discover that, despite its connection with the world of the supernatural, the subject of magic through gramarye had a lighter side. One character says to a wizard in the *Townley Mystery Plays* of 1460, "Cowthe [could] ye, by youre gramery, rech us a drynke, I shuld be more mery."

An altered form of grammar, *glamour*, introduced into literature by Sir Walter Scott, originally represented another type of magic, a "fascination by the power of the eye," once called *glamour-might* and *eye-biting*. Jamieson linked magic with the eyes in defining glamour: "The supposed influence of a charm on the eye, causing it to see objects differently from what they really are." In an 1830 letter, Scott implicated the gypsies in this murky subject: "This species of witchcraft is well known in Scotland as the glamour, or *deceptio visus*, and was supposed to be a special attribute of the Gipsies." In his writings, Scott used glamour in a chivalrous though sober fashion, as in these lines from *Lay of the Last Minstrel:*

> It had much of glamour might,
> Could make a ladye seem a knight;
> The cobwebs on a dungeon wall
> Seem tapistry in lordly hall;
> And youth seem age, and age seem youth—
> All was delusion, nought was truth.

Shakespeare was well aware of this kind of enchantment, writing in *Titus Andronicus*,

> . . . fettered in amorous chains,
> And faster bound to Aaron's charming eyes
> Than is Prometheus tied to Caucasus.

Not until the late nineteenth century did glamour begin to denote an explicitly sexual feminine attraction, although that quality was alluded to in Victorian "novelettes," such as one with the alluring title *Held In Bondage*, which melodramatically stated, "I know how quickly the glamour fades in the test of intercourse."

DUNSMAN * Disciple of a school of thought that supported such intellectually indefensible notions as the Immaculate Conception. This group was ridiculed as a circle of fussy "dunsmen," a name shortened by critics to *dunces*. Dunsman was coined after the name of John Duns Scotus, a thirteenth-century Scottish philosopher, whose brilliance as a logician earned him a place in fourteenth-century university textbooks. However, after his death, followers such as one satirized in *Hudibras* attempted to continue his work with only limited success:

> He was a shrewd philosopher,
> And had read ev'ry text and gloss over;
> Whatever skeptic could enquire for,
> For every why he had a wherefore.

From dunsman also came the well-known "dunce-cap," used into the twentieth century to humiliate schoolchildren who were likewise unable to demonstrate intelligence. A dunsman's intellect, as well as that of the school, was ridiculed in *Hudibras:*

He knew what's what, and that's as high
As metaphysic wit can fly,
In school-divinity as able
As he that hight irreffagable [calls himself irrefutable];
A second Thomas [Aquinas] or at once,
To name them all, another Duns.

According to the *Oxford English Dictionary*, during the seventeenth century a *dunce-table* was "a table for duller or poorer students in some Inns of Court." A saying of Benjamin Franklin with application to dunsmen is found in *Poor Richard's Almanack* of 1734: "A learned blockhead is a greater blockhead than an ignorant one."

7. *Fun and Games*

Tup-Running, Bladderskates, and Karrows

CACHPULE * Ancestral name for tennis or a tennis court, used throughout the sixteenth century, and based partially on the Old French *cache*, an incursion. The forerunner of this early form of European racket sports, played at first using only the hands, originated in French monasteries nearly a millennia ago. This game was outlawed by the Church because of the interest it evoked, but was eventually adopted instead by aristocrats and kings, such as England's Henry VIII, who appropriately dubbed it "royal tennis." In 1664, Pepys commented on the indispensable need for flattery in order to "win" at this sport:

"To the tennis court and there saw the king play at tennis . . . but to see how the king's play was extolled without any cause at all was a loathsome sight." The first courts, which were like one-hundred-foot-long squash courts, featured a roof, asymmetrical walls, and windows called "grilles" at the receiver's end that functioned as hazards and goals for scoring. Early balls, made of leather stuffed with dog hair or cotton, were struck with handmade rackets that varied wildly in design. In 1607, Cleland editorialized about the game:

> The tennis court, whereby I would have you to recreate your mind and exercise your body sometimes; for besides pleasure it preserveth your health, in so far as it moveth every part of the body. Nevertheless, I approve not those who are ever in the tennis court like nackets [boy who served or sold the balls] and heat themselves so much that they rather breed than expell sickness; nor yet commend I those who rail at the Tennis-keeper's score, and that have banded away the greater part of their wealth in playing great and many sets. It is both a hurt and a shame for a nobleman to be so eager in that play.

The word tennis might have developed in relation to the now submerged island of *Tinnis* in the Nile Delta, where cotton was grown and a fine cotton fabric that might have been used in making balls—called *tissus de tennis*—was manufactured. Or the name might have been derived from *tenetz*, an Anglo-Norman word accented on the second syllable, meaning "Take this!"— possibly a challenge from the server to his opponent.

———

GLEEK * A variety of sixteenth- to nineteenth-century enjoyment-oriented activities, the roots of which extend from the Old English words *glig*, mirth, and *gleowian*, jest. A *gleekman* was a professional entertainer such as a mimic who commonly evoked *gle*, an Anglo-Saxon word for "pleasure," while *glee-men* were singers and minstrels, who would later form "glee-clubs." By the fifteenth century, gleek had a variety of meanings, including a trick or practical joke, usually at someone else's expense, called "giving one the gleek." It is probably in this

context that Shakespeare wrote in *Romeo and Juliet:* "I'll give you no money, on my faith, but the gleek." In *A Midsummer-Night's Dream*, Bottom boasts of his wittiness, "Nay, I can gleek on occasion." A favorite card game of one of Henry VIII's wives, Catherine of Aragon, was Gleek, the object of which was to collect a set of three cards of the same rank. Nares cited the rules of this complex, forty-four-card forerunner of the children's game of Fish, which encouraged wagering, from Witt's 1640 *Recreations:*

> The deuces and trois are thrown out of the pack; each person has twelve cards dealt to him and eight are left for the stock, seven of which may be bought by the players, the eighth is the turn-up card, which belongs to the dealer. The cards had nicknames: the ace of trumps being called Tib, the knave, Tom, and the four, Tiddie; each of these is paid for, to him who holds it, by the other two.

Samuel Pepys wrote candidly of playing Gleek in the 1660s: "My Aunt Wright and my wife and I to cards, she teaching us to playe at gleek; but I love not my aunt so far as to be troubled with it." His attitude toward the game changed, however, a few weeks later after he had walked away from the table a winner of big money—nine shillings: "The most I ever won in my life. I pray God it may not tempt me to play again." Later, based on this game, a gleek became a trio of anything, and *Dutch-gleek* became a facetious term for alcohol consumption.

———

GAMMON ✳ A term still commonly heard in English butcher shops, meaning a ham or pork haunch, taken from the Old French *gambon*, and related to the modern French *jambe*, a leg, and *jambon*, ham. Gammon appears to have stemmed from Middle English *gamen*, or hunting game. At one time the quantity of pork was valued as much as the quality, as is illustrated by this passage from the 1822 *Cottage Economy* by William Cobbett:

> Make your pig quite fat by all means. The last bushel, even if he sat as he eat, is the most profitable. If he can walk two hundred yards at a time, he is not well fatted. Lean bacon is the most wasteful thing that any family can use. The man that cannot [dine] on solid fat bacon . . . wants the sweet sauce of labour, or is fit for the hospital.

Roasted gammons called "bartholomew pigges" were a major attraction on Saint Bartholomew's Day, "sold piping hot, and ostentatiously displayed to excite the appetites of passengers." On August 24th, from 1133 until 1855, a fair was held in honor of this patron saint of butchers, cheese merchants, and tanners, just outside the northern gates of London in Smithfield. Nares implied that the Puritans railed against this porky treat for its blasphemous name, adding that eating it was considered the "spice of adultery." An eyewitness account of 1641 reported the hubbub that generally took place at these fairs:

Hither resort people of all sorts and conditions. It is remarkable and worth your observation to beholde and
heare the strange sights and confused noise in the faire.
Here a knave in a foole's coate, with a trumpet sounding
or a drumme beating, invites you to see his puppets;
there, a rogue like a wild woodman in an antick shape
like an Incubus, desires you to view his motion. On the
other side, hocus pocus with three yards of tape or ribbin
in's hand, showing his art of legerdemaine, to the admi-
ration and astonishment of a company of cockoloaches.

In John Stephen's 1631 *New Essayes and Characters*, we are led to
think that people bought mainly religious literature on this
day: "Like a bookseller's shoppe on Bartholomew's Day at London, the stalls [out front] are so adorn'd with bibles and
prayer-books that nothing is left within but heathen knowledge." It was perhaps partially a result of these fairs that a late
seventeenth-century verb form of gammon developed, meaning
to deceive simple people; by 1800, gammon had become synonymous with *poppycock* or the modern *baloney*. In this regard
Dickens wrote in the *Pickwick Papers*, "Some people maintain
that an Englishman's house is his castle. That's gammon!"

BLADDERSKATE * An "indistinct or indiscreet talker,"
according to Jamieson, the first part of which was taken from
blaedre, the Anglo-Saxon forerunner of the urinary bladder. Medieval court jokesmiths typically inflated these balloonlike
sacks, meant as a take-off on their own character, and tied them
to a wand called a *bauble*. This prop was used to playfully
threaten and strike their audiences (called "flailing the bladder") while they sang, juggled, told stories, performed magic
tricks, and engaged in acts of comical self-deprecation, such as
controlled flatulence. In 1596, Thomas Lodge was obviously not

amused when he wrote the following unflattering profile of a jester in *Wit's Miserie:*

> This fellow in person is comely, in apparel courtly, but in behavior a very ape, and no man; his studye is to coine bitter jeastes, or to show antique motions, or to sing baudie sonnets and ballads. Give him a little wine in his head, he is continually flearing and making of mouths; he laughs intemperately at every occasion and dances about the house, leaps over the tables, outskips men's heads, trips up his companion's heels, burns sacke with a candle and has all the features of a Lord of Misrule in the countrie.

Jesters, as they could say things that others could not, were sometimes powerful players in court politics. They used their access to the king and his ministers to influence decisions, often on someone's behalf. Their rarified blend of intelligence and wit was lauded by Viola in *Twelfth Night:*

> This fellow's wise enough to play the fool,
> And to do that craves a kind of wit:
> He must observe their mood on whom he jests,
> The quality of persons, and the time,
> And like the haggard, check at every feather
> That comes before his eye. This is a practice
> As full of labour as a wise man's art.

From blaedre came several other derisive terms, including the adjective *bladdered,* meaning proud or "puffed up," *blateroon,* a blabbermouth, and *blithering idiot,* which is still in use.

SCATCHES * Originally, stilts worn from the early sixteenth to the nineteenth century when walking in filthy places, probably based on a Greek root from which also sprang the odd eighteenth-century word, *scatomancy,* meaning "fecal fortune-telling." From scatches, the Dutch created *schaats* in the mid-1600s, and the English *skates*, contrivances originally fashioned from the lower leg bones of cows. Although the change in sense from stilts to skates is not well understood, Wedgewood's nineteenth-century dictionary managed to link their

functions: "The point in which stilts and skates agree is that they are both contrivances for increasing the length of stride." In the twelfth century, Fitz-Stephen wrote of young people whom he watched using animal bones to increase their skateless "ice-gliding" speed: "Taking in their hands poles shod with iron, which at times they strike against the ice, they are carried along with as great rapidity as a bird flying or a bolt discharged from a cross-bow." Samuel Pepys was also fascinated by skaters, writing in his 1662 diary, "Over [in] the park, where I first in my life, it being a great frost, did see people sliding with their skeates, which is a very pretty art." The use of scatches appears to have taken its toll, especially among eager novices. During the seventeenth and eighteenth centuries, it was not uncommon for a number of Londoners to drown in a single day as a result of skating on thin ice. It became such a popular and dangerous pastime, in fact, that Saint Lidwyna was resuscitated as the patron saint of skaters.

KARROWS * Hard-core fourteenth- to eighteenth-century Irish gamesters, portrayed by Holinshed's *Chronicles* as "a brotherhood of karrowes that prefer to play at chartes [cards] all the yere long, and make it their onely occupation." Richard Stanyhurst, a sixteenth-century historian, spotlighted these characters, who gave the expression "winner take all" a new meaning, as the karrows would "plaie awaie mantle [clothing] and all to bare skin and then trusse themselves in straw or leaves." Consequently, they were often in debt to *gullgroupers*, usurers who lent money to gamblers. Because of debt-collection practices, the eighteenth-century *Rothenburg Statute Book* dictated specifically that Prussian gamblers could only lose what they had come into the gaming room with, which included "outer garments only." Karrows were apt to use weighted dice called *fulhams*, after their place of manufacture near London, or *low-men*, crafted to produce low numbers, and the not quite cubical *langrets*, which tended to come up threes and fours. *The Compleat Gamester* mentioned the construction of another type of false dice:

> Bristle-dice are filled for their purpose by sticking a hog's bristle so . . . in the dice that they shall run high or low, as they please; this bristle must be strong and short, by which means the bristle bends [but] will not lie on that side, but will be tript over.

In 1596, Spencer wrote of karrows as "lewd and dishonest," and characterized them as

> a kinde of people that wander up and downe to gentlemen's houses, living onely upon cardes and dice, the which, though they have little or nothing of their owne,

yet will play for much money, which if they winne, they
waste most lightly, and if they lose, they pay as slenderly,
but make recompense with one stealth or another. . . .
[Their] only hurt is not that they themselves are idle
lossells, but that through gaming they draw others to
like lewdness and idleness.

A 1702 issue of *The English Post* cited a supreme example of
gaming fever: "An inditement is presented against a person in
Westminster for playing away his wife to another man, which
was done with her consent." Groom-porters, officers of the English royal household, were appointed to distribute honest playing cards and evenly weighted square dice, as well as settle the
disputes that inevitably arose. These supposedly impartial

overseers, however, proved as corruptible as any, and were soon
running their own disreputable gaming establishments, as we
read in one of John Evelyn's 1668 diary entries: "I saw deep
and prodigious gaming at the groom-porter's, vast heaps of gold
squandered away in a vain and profuse manner." The prevailing
attitude toward gaming and honor among aristocrats is revealed
in these lines from the eighteenth-century play, *The Gamester*,
as Hector admonishes Sir Thomas, who has reneged on a gambling debt:

"How, not pay, Sir. Why, Sir, among gentlemen that debt is look'd upon the most just of any. You may cheat widows, orphans, tradesmen without a blush, but a debt of honour, Sir, must be paid."

BEARGARDEN * Beginning in the twelfth century, the London setting on the south bank of the Thames allocated to exhibition of the Roman-inspired *bear-baiting*. This cruel sport, which involved setting dogs on a bear for spectator amusement,

was considered a "very rude and nasty pleasure," by Samuel Pepys, yet jocularly called *bear's-college* by Ben Jonson. It was mentioned in *Hudibras:*

> 'Twas an old way of recreating,
> Which learned butchers call bear-baiting.

Queen Elizabeth, who enjoyed watching jousting, boxing, falconry, and stag-hunting, commonly witnessed animal-baiting here, along with other dignitaries such as her queen-to-be half sister, Mary, as we learn from Chambers's *Book of Days:*

> Elizabeth took especial delight in seeing the [baiting]. On the 25th of May, 1559, the French ambassadors were

brought to court . . . and after a splendid dinner were en-
tertained with the baiting of bears and bulls. . . . The dip-
lomats were so gratified, that her majesty never failed to
provide a similar show for any foreign visitors she wished
to honour.

Although baiting was clearly deemed a sport, Hazlitt believed
there might once have been method in the madness, at least
for the baiting of the more edible bulls:

A considerable body of authentic testimony exists to
show that this apparently cruel amusement was due to a
theory on the part of our ancestors that the process rendered the flesh more tender, and some of the Leet Courts
in England imposed a fine of three shillings, four pence
on every butcher who killed a bullock unbaited.

A May 1667 diary entry of Pepys broadened the parameters of
a prizefight: "Abroad and stopped at the Bear-garden stairs,
there to see a prize[fight] . . . [between] a butcher and a wa-
terman. The former had the better all along, till by and by the
latter dropped his sword." Figuratively, beargarden came to
denote any tumultuous scene of argument, confusion, or general
commotion. The expression "bear-garden discourse," rude language from the late seventeenth to early nineteenth centuries,
was also derived from this activity. Children participated in a
rough game called "badger-the-bear," based on bear baiting,
wherein one boy on hands and knees represented a bear while
another boy played his "bearherd" or keeper, defending him
from attacks.

———————

SCARAMOUCH * Late fourteenth-century term for en-
counters between groups of soldiers, which has come down to
us as *skirmish*. The French *escarmouche*, from which was created
the Middle English *scarmuche*, a fencing engagement, was

spawned by the Italian *scaramuccia*. Scaramouch also became an enduring verb that meant "acting in a cowardly manner," based upon a character of this name from early Italian satirical comedy who was often pummeled for his knavish actions. A traveling actor calling himself Scaramuzza, who developed a lazy, swaggering character intended to ridicule Spanish nobility, was described by Blount as "a famous Italian 'zani' or mountebank, who acted here in England in 1673." Skirmish was later broadened into the realm of sports, where the nineteenth-century rugby word *scrummage* and the American football *scrimmage* descended from the robust English "foot-bal skermysches," a 1719 description of which we hear from Misson: "In winter, footballs is a useful and charming exercise. It is a leather ball about as big as one's head, fill'd with wind. This is kick'd about from one t'other in the streets by him that can get at it, and this is all the art of it."

Richard Carew, in his 1602 *Survey of Cornwall*, downplayed the long-term significance of sports injuries in writing about the sport of hurling:

> The ball in this play may be compared to an infernal spirit; for whosoever catcheth it, fareth straightways like a mad man, struggling and fighting with those who go about to hold him. . . . You shall see them retiring home as from a pitched battle, with bloody pates, bones broken and out of joint, and such bruises as serve to shorten their days; yet all is good play, and never attorney or coroner troubled.

Football skirmishes were formally forbidden by a Scottish statute of 1424, as Elgot, a local governor explained: "Foote balle, wherein is nothinge but beastly furie and exstreme violence . . . is to be put in perpetuall silence." Even the virile and robust Henry VIII, who jousted, wielded a sword, executed monks, political dissenters, and wives, and frequently tired out half a dozen horses in a fourteen-hour day of hunting, banned football as "too violent."

TUP-RUNNING * An ancient rural sport practiced at funeral wakes and fairs in Derbyshire. The name was an imported version of the Belgian *tulpe*, "to strike or push, as a ram," and was used especially in Suffolk and Norfolk. In this raucous form of entertainment, which presumably followed heavy drinking, the tail of a ram, once known as a *tup*, was soaped and greased with lard. The animal was then allowed to run wild among the participants, who, in order to claim this feisty quadruped as a prize, had to hold fast to its tail. Predictable accompaniments

to this activity may be reflected by alternate definitions of *tup*, including "to butt," and "to bow to someone before drinking." A related but more dangerous activity is found in Butcher's 1775 *Survey of Stamford*, where bull-running was practiced:

> It was performed just the day six weeks before Christmas. The butchers of the town . . . provide the wildest bull they can get; proclamation is made by the common bellman of the town that each shut-up their shop doors and

gates . . . [and] the bull is turned out; men, women and children of all sorts and sizes, with all the dogs in the town promiscuously running after him with their bull clubs spattering dirt in each other's faces that one would think them to be so many Furies started out of Hell for the punishment of Cerberus.

Tup later connoted carnal knowledge of a woman.

DRAW-GLOVES * Parlor game played from the fourteenth to eighteenth centuries. Apparently the object was to draw one's gloves off before the other player when certain agreed-upon words were spoken. Several accounts, including this one from Herrick's *Hesperides*, implied an amorous reason for this game's longevity:

> At Draw-Gloves we'l play,
> And prethee, let's lay
> A wager, and let it be this:
> Who first to the summe
> Of twenty shall come
> Shall have for his winning a kisse.

This game was engaged in by members of the opposite sex, at least one of whom generally had what was called a "*love-tooth* in

the head," that is, an inclination to love. Often the next step for couples such as this was to "look [for] babies in the eyes," meaning to look so closely at the other's eyes as to be capable of seeing their own reflection in the other's pupil, which was apparently mistaken for Cupid. With this phrase, Beaumont and Fletcher, in their play *The Loyal Subject*, pose the amorous question,

> Can ye look babies, sister,
> In the young gallants' eyes,
> And twirl their bandstrings?

8. The Staff of Life
Dilligrout, Wayzgoose, and Uzzle-Pye

HORSE-BREAD * Coarse mixture of bran, alfalfa, beans, vegetable trimmings, and fodder, disclosed in sixteenth-century writings, which was made by bakers to be fed to pampered ponies to enliven and strengthen them, much as oats are now. This equine dietary supplement was formed into "great household peck loaves—to avoid crust" before cooking, and despite its original purpose, horse-bread was quietly mixed into dishes or baked into breads and discreetly served to unsuspecting travelers by unscrupulous innkeepers. This practice apparently became so widespread that a fourteenth-century "purity law" of Edward III mandated that horse-bread be served exclusively to horses and made "only of beans and peas, without other mixture." In olden times, bakers were put in stocks for adulterating loaves and, because of their persistent temptation to cheat, a variety of legislation was enacted. As late as the 1860s,

> Bakers making or selling or exposing to sale, bread made wholly or partially of peas or beans or potatoes, or any other sort of corn or grain other than wheat, without being marked with a large Roman M (which means meal) [is] to forfeit for every pound weight of such bread, a fine not exceeding ten shillings or one month's imprisonment.

One explanation for how another type of coarse bread, *pumpernickel*, received its name is that Napoleon, upon sampling this Prussian staple, pronounced it in French, *"pain pour Nicole,"* literally bread for his horse, Nicole. Unfortunately for the story, the word pumpernickel, which when translated from German meant roughly "devil's flatulence," appears to have existed since the 1660s—well before Napoleon's time.

———————

MOCTEROOF * Term of obscure origin used in the mid-1800s for the craft of *frubbishing* or dressing up damaged fruits and vegetables used by produce *kramers* or peddlers. Beeswax, for example, was applied to chestnuts by shaking the two together in a box. Mayhew recorded some other nineteenth-century tricks of the trade used by a shady London costermonger:

> "I've boiled lots of oranges," chuckled one man, "and sold 'em to Irish hawkers as wasn't wide awake, for stunning big uns. The boiling swells the oranges and so makes 'em look finer ones, but it spoils them, for it takes out the juice. People can't find that out though until it's too late. I boiled the oranges only a few minutes, and three or four dozen at a time." Oranges thus prepared will not keep, and any Irishwoman, tricked as were my informant's customers, is astonished to find her stock of oranges turn dark-coloured and worthless in forty-eight hours.

Mayhew continued his exposé with the example of another peddler, who rationalized a practice called "topping up," or putting the best produce on top:

> "Topping up," said a fruit dealer to me, "is the principal thing, and we are perfectly justified in it. You ask any coster that knows the world, and he'll tell you that all the salesmen in the markets tops up. It's only making the best of it."

He concluded with two other secrets: "Filberts they bake to make them look more brown and ripe. Prunes they boil to give them a plumper and finer appearance." A seventeenth-century *mangonist* was a market person who "tricked up" various types of inferior quality goods, such as fruits and vegetables. This

term was inspired by a sinister verb, *to mangonize*, or to pamper slaves with extra food and rest to make them appear stronger and healthier in preparation for their sale.

GROANING-CHEESE * Large special cheese, or *milk-meat*, originally from Northern England that, along with a *groaning-cake*, was provided, until the nineteenth century, by a husband in the interest of soothing his wife during childbirth. Hazlitt wrote about the groaning-cheese:

> It is customary at Oxford to cut the cheese in the middle when the child is born, and so by degrees form it into a large ring, through which the child must be passed on the day of the christening. It was not unusual to preserve for many years, I know not for what superstitious intent, pieces of the groaning-cake.

Harland illuminated another aspect of this custom: "Throughout the north of England, the first cut of the sick wife's cheese, or groaning cheese, is taken and laid under the pillows of young women to cause them to dream of their lovers." As might be expected, to wash down the groaning-cheese and groaning-cake was brewed a *groaning-drink*, also called a *bed-ale*, served in celebration of the new arrival, along with *blithemeat* in Scotland.

Any remains of the cheese and cake were kept for subsequent callers, and every visitor was expected to taste them. For support during their delivery, women availed themselves of a *groaning-chair*, perhaps called such because, if it didn't creak before this ordeal, it was likely to do so afterward.

NONSHENCH * Compound Middle English term derived from the Old English *non*, noon, and *schenche*, which meant, according to Skeat, "a pouring out or distribution of drink, accompanied by noon-meat." By the seventeenth century, *nuncheon*, as it became known, was also referred to as a *nuntion*, *noonshine*, and *noonchin*, as well as *nunchings*, which were simple midday foods. Meanwhile, nobles commonly enjoyed "noonscape" meals, known by the telltale name of "drynkyngs." Ash's dictionary of 1775 added another possible meaning for *nunchin*, used colloquially: "A piece of victuals eaten between meals." As late as the 1890s, nuncheon could mean a light morning or afternoon meal, but disappeared around the turn of the century. In Thomas Urquhart's seventeenth-century book, *Rabelais*, he mused: "Some say there is . . . no dinner like a lawyer's, no afternoon nuncheon like a vintner's."

Lunch initially signified a lump or hunk of cheese, bread, or meat, as well as a bunch of grapes, while *lunchin* later came to mean a snack between more substantial meals. Dr. Johnson's 1755 dictionary defined lunch as "As much food as one's hands can hold," and he ventured to guess that lunch was there-

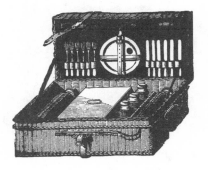

fore descended from "clutch" or an older "clunch," not luncheon. Despite their uncanny similarity, luncheon and nuncheon were kept quite distinct for centuries and were sometimes even used in the same sentence or verse, as a nineteenth-century couplet from Robert Browning demonstrates:

> So munch on, crunch on, take your nuncheon,
> Breakfast, supper, dinner, luncheon.

Until the twentieth century, luncheon was, by and large, upper-class fare, while those who earned a living generally only snacked at lunchtime, except perhaps on Sundays.

FLITCH * A side of various game animals, from as long ago as the early eighth century, and recently applied only to bacon. The phrase, "to bring home the bacon," developed during the fourteenth century in the Essex County town of Dunmow, England. Dunmow records show that a noblewoman attempted to encourage marital contentment by offering a gammon, or side of bacon called a *Dunmow flitch*, to any couple who would swear that for the past year they had not had a household brawl or wished themselves unmarried. The claimant couple was sometimes verbally examined before a panel of six bachelors and six unmarried maidens. This flitch became a symbol of domestic happiness but, by 1772, only eight of these prizes were awarded—and those to men only. An abridged version of the oath itself reads:

> You shall swear by custom of confession,
> If ever you made a nuptual transgression,
> Or, since the parish-clerk said Amen,
> You wish'd yourselves unmarried again,
> But continued true in thought and desire
> As when you joined hands in the quire.
> A whole gammon of bacon you shall receive,
> And bear it hence with love and good leave;
> For this is our custom at Dunmow well known,
> Though the pleasure be ours, the bacon's your own.

The rough-hewn proverb "Do not fetch your wife from Dunmow, for so you may bring home two sides of a sow," was mentioned by Howell in 1659, as well as writers of the fourteenth century, including Chaucer. A brief revival of marital felicity apparently took place in 1902 when fourteen couples applied for the award—though only two qualified.

SALVOR * Medieval servant of royalty or nobles, who was once beckoned by the unappetizing title of *sewer*. His primary duty was to sample the food and drink prepared for his masters, who had a *back-fear*, or paranoia, about assassination by poisons such as *aqua Tofana*, which contained arsenic. Salvor, which originally meant "savior," was descended from the Latin *salvus*, "safe," and served as the root for *salvage*, *salvation*, and *salve*, something which might save one from pain. Later spelled *salver*, it came to indicate the silver tray onto which the tested victuals were placed before being offered, first to the taster and afterward to the master. By the mid-seventeenth century, this platter became less necessary and more ornamental, and was represented by Blount as "A new fashioned peece of wrought plate, broad and flat . . . used in giving beer or other liquid thing, to save the carpit or cloathes from drops." Before salver was transplanted into English, according to Minsheu's *Spanish Dictionary* of 1623, it was used in the Spanish phrase, *hacer salva*, "to taste meat or drinke . . . as they do with princes." In the sixteenth century, a similar form of protection was sought from fine glassware, such as Venetian crystal, which, it was believed, would break and thereby protect the drinker, if tainted liquids were poured into it.

DILLIGROUT * Dish of porridge prepared in noblemen's kitchens for the coronation banquets of English kings from 1662 to 1820. In return for performing this type of culinary service, the retention of their English estates (such as Addington manor in Surrey) was secured. In earlier times, nobles were each often required to provide food for the king and his staff on one or more days per year. Certainly this cooking was a mere inconvenience compared with the responsibilities of some coastal land-holders, as we learn in Williamson's *Curious Survivals:*

> There are certain noblemen who are still known as "Ad-mirals of the Coast," and who, by reason of the possession of estates bordering on the sea-coast, had duties given to them to overlook the defences of their particular districts. Upon the master laid the burden of seeing that the guard of the coasts was properly maintained and supervised, and they were, in Tudor times, frequently called upon to sup-ply ships and men.

Some of the roots of this feudally founded food preparation custom are found in the fourteenth-century word *potew*, a dish cooked in an earthenware pot that was broken after its contents were served to royalty, to prevent its use by a person of inferior social status. Dilligrout's prefix, *dilli*, probably referred to a prominent spice in this recipe, while *grout*, a derivative of the Anglo-Saxon *grut*, had meant a coarse meal of hulled barley *groats* or *gruel* since at least the eighth century. Dilligrout pre-sumably had a more delectable flavor and consistency than the mortar used for finishing tile, called simply *grout*, whose name it inspired seven hundred years later.

FARCTATE * The condition of being bloated or full fol-lowing a large meal. This term hails from the Latin *farcire*, to stuff, which also gave rise to the thirteenth-century *farcemeat*, seventeenth-century *farcement*, and the still-used French *farci*, all spicy stuffings for meat dishes. In her 1845 *Modern Cookery*, Eliza Acton dourly implied that another derivative, *forcemeat*, at least prepared English style, might have had more in com-mon with horsemeat than a rhyming name: "The coarse and unpalatable compounds so constantly met with under the denomination of forcemeat, even at tables otherwise tolerably served, show with how little attention they are prepared."

Smith's *The Compleat Housewife* contained a recipe for "a good vomit," which undoubtedly provided many moments of relief among the English:

> Take two ounces of the finest white alum, beat it small, put it into better than half a pint of new milk, set it on a slow fire till the milk is turned clear; let it stand a quarter of an hour; strain it off and drink it just warm; it will give three or four vomits, and is very safe.

In earlier times, uncontrolled feasting was rationalized by the common belief, alluded to in *Twelfth Night*, that occasional excess helped one achieve self-control:

> If music be the food of love, play on;
> Give me excess of it, that, surfeiting,
> The appetite may sicken, and so die.

Conversation may have waited until after many Irish meals, if there is any truth to their old adage "Men are like bagpipes: No sound comes from them till they're full." Aubrey's 1686 *Remaines of Gentilisme* explains why, in Sussex, snake skin was added to gourmands' head apparel: "The Sussexians doe weare them for Hatt-bands, which they say doe preserve them from the gripeing of the Gutts." A seventh-century abbot, Saint Renovatus, is remembered for his treatment of a gluttonous monk at his monastery at Cauliana. After several unsuccessful approaches, he allowed his charge to have an unlimited intake of food and drink. The monk responded by consuming enormous meals until he "was conscience-struck." The farctate friar confessed his abuses to the abbot and died a few days later.

CUPBOARD-LOVE * Literary embellishment, combining emotional insincerity and gastronomic desire, denoting people who valued both matter over mind and the ability of others to satisfy their physical needs. This "meal-ticket" relationship, which might easily have developed between an estate's cook and a chambermaid, is illustrated by the following lines from the seventeenth-century *Poor Robin's Almanack:*

> A cupboard love is seldom true,
> A love sincere is found in few;
> But 'tis high time for folks to marry,
> When women woo, lest things miscarry.

The 1665 *Roxburghe Ballads* included an early form of cupboard-love: "And all for the love of cubbard." A person exhibiting cupboard-love might also have been known as a *belly-friend* two hundred years ago, or a *backfriend* in the fifteenth century. Sir George Dasent, in his 1874 *Tales from Norse Traditions*, first used the cupboard to represent something forbidden or illicit, as in a *cupboard lover*, just as people today use "closet" for the same allusion.

NUMBLES * Anglo-Saxon word meaning "animal intestines and internal organs," borrowed from Old French in the fourteenth century. Known also as *trillibub*, these pieces were commonly eaten by peasants and servants in dishes such as *garbage pye*, a deep-dish pastry made of giblets, eggs, and sugar, or *haggis*, a viscera-stuffed animal stomach. Typically, the choicest *pulpatoons*, or tidbits, of wild game were claimed by the hunter bagging the prey, who consumed them with his eldest son and

hunting buddies, while the less palatable parts went to humbler local residents. Anthropologists say this custom is an ironic reversal from Saxon times when hunters valued internal organs as the essence of the animal's spirit. Not uncommonly, they ate the heart, liver, and kidneys ceremonially in the field, before bringing the rest of the carcass home for a multitude of uses, including two mentioned by Butler:

> For guts, some write, ere they are sodden [boiled],
> Are fit for music, or for pudden.

English ambivalence toward "innards" continued, evidenced by Pepys's 1665 complaint to his diary about the fare at a dinner party: "He did give us the meanest dinner of beef, shoulder and umbles of venison."

A vegetarian version of numbles, an unusual dish called *hastlet* (from Old French *hastelet*, meat roasted on a spit, and Latin *hasta*, the spit itself), artfully employed fresh and dried fruits and a variety of nuts to simulate roasted intestines, internal organs, and genitalia, called "tenderlings," of wild game such as deer and boar. This favorite among hunters was valued largely for its visual appeal, and often served alongside its meat counterpart. A special delicacy related to tenderlings was known as "dainties," and consisted of deer testicles served with sweet and sour sauce, alluded to in *Love's Labour's Lost:* "He hath never fed of the dainties that are bred in a book." Numbles was corrupted over time to *umble* and later *humble*, and by 1830 had become part of the phrase "eating humble pie," which now implies an apologetic demeanor or state. Two similar Latin words appear to be related to humble, *lumulus*, a loin, and *humilis*, low or mean.

***

U Z Z L E - P Y E * More medieval spectacle than food, this dish was a crowd-pleaser. The *Oxford Dictionary of Nursery Rhymes* notes that an Italian cookbook of 1549 offered a recipe for making "pyes so that birds may be alive in them and flie out when it is cut up." The crust was prepared with temporary contents, such as dried beans, to weigh down the bottom crust and support the lid while baking, and then emptied. After baking, small live birds such as blackbirds were then tethered inside without being harmed. At an appropriate moment, the top crust was removed, causing a commotion inside the pie, as illustrated by the lines from *Sing a Song of Sixpence*, "when the pie was opened, the birds began to sing." According to eighteenth-century historian John Nott, when increased drama was desired, the birds were left unsecured and allowed to fly around the room in order "to put out the candles and so cause a diverting Hurley-Burley among the guests in the dark." Not until the 1500s did pie filling generally include fruit, as it commonly does today.

SMELL-FEASTE * A mannerless *belly-god* or *gutling*, commonly depicted from the 1540s to 1700, who appeared un-invited to share in a feast. In the thirteenth century, books of etiquette were first published in an attempt to elevate the dining experience by eliminating various types of boorish behavior such as this. Such books suggested that diners avoid wiping their fingers and mouth with their bread. Using three fingers

to eat and the thumb to butter bread was the mark of a gentleman, while employing all five proved one to be a rustic. Partially gnawed bones, it was recommended by Erasmus, should be thrown on the floor, preferably in a corner, rather than put back on the serving platter. Scratching fleas, lice, or one's groin at the table, and *slottering*, the making of snorting, animal-like chewing sounds, were similarly discouraged, as was *sooming*, defined by Charles Mackay as "to drink a long draught, with a sucking noise of the mouth, as if in great thirst or with great relish."

A related eighteenth-century Lincolnshire county word, *anshum-scranchum*, indicated an uncomfortable situation in which a tableful of hungry diners was served an insufficient quantity of food, and awkwardly attempted to satiate themselves quickly without appearing too uncivilized. In *The Gentlewoman's Companion* of 1675, Hannah Woolley tried to teach readers how to behave in case they found themselves in an anchum-scranchum:

> Do not venture to eat meat so hot that the tears stand in your eyes, for that thereby you betray your intolerable greediness; neither fill your mouth so full that your cheeks shall swell like a pair of Scotch bagpipes. Gnaw no bones with your teeth, nor suck . . . the marrow.

Although *tooth-music*, the sound of people chewing, was not uncommon at a meal, *squackett*, disagreeable gutteral sounds, became less acceptable over time.

WAYZGOOSE * An annual gathering, originally of printers and their families, where goose may have been provided by the master; described by Bailey in 1749 as "entertainment given to journeymen, at the beginning of winter." Bailey suggested that *wayz* once meant a bundle of straw, making the bird a "stubble goose," one fattened late in the year in harvested fields. This practice can be traced to at least as long ago as the fourteenth-century, when it was depicted by Chaucer in the *Cook's Prologue*. Shipley felt that a more plausible time for this dinner get-together was late summer "about Bartholomew-tide [August 24], marking the beginning of work by candle-light." By the early 1800s, the *beanfeast* had largely replaced the wayzgoose as a budget-minded version of this assembly, whose name was possibly derived from *bene*, a Latin word for solicitation, and the root of "benediction," as a collection was often taken up at these meals. In all likelihood though, beanfeast was simply drawn from the most common type of main dish generally served, as we learn from W. T. Vincent's 1875 *Warlike Woolwich:*

> The holiday on the second Saturday in July, which is a special and extra holiday known as Bean-feast day, and is usually spent in excursions to some country place and a dinner, at which beans form an indispensable dish.

An 1805 issue of *Sporting Magazine* indicated that beans were not the only dish found at these wind-generating congregations: "A Gentleman Taylor, celebrated for his liberality, gave a rich treat to his men, at his occasional country residence. It was called a Bean Feast; but, exclusive of the beans, the table literally groaned with bacon." Regardless of what the timing and menu happened to be, the wayzgoose served as an early model for the now commonplace "company picnic."

9. *Love Is Blind*

Amobers, Stangsters, and Piggesnyes

BRIDELOPE * Earliest English word for a marriage custom, dating back to A.D. 950 when it was called *brydlopa*. Part of this custom, called the "run for the bride-door," was an ancient tradition in which the bride was both symbolically and physically swept off on horseback to her husband's home by him and sometimes a helper who was later known as the "best man." The Anglo-Saxon root word *wedd* ("to gamble, wager") first referred to livestock or other payment by the groom to the bride's father, as a more civilized alternative to abduction. In the seventeenth century, before it became associated with romantic images, elopement was a legal term for the act of a woman who leaves her husband and, according to Blount, "dwells with an adulterer, by which she shall lose her dower." As a symbol of resistance, the well-prepared Saxon bride's wedding attire often included knives, which she "gracefully hung from her girdle." John Heywood listed other bridal equipment in his 1545 work, *The Four Ps:*

> Silke swathbonds, ribbands, and sleeve-laces,
> Girdles, knives, purses and pin-cases.
> Fortune doth give these knives to you,
> To cut the thred of love if't be not true.

Bridesmaids were originally a maid's closest friends who might attempt to defend her from an unwanted groom and make sure she didn't panic and run off, especially in arranged marriages. In a custom known as "chaining the path," the bride was hidden or disguised when the groom's party came for her, as we learn from Burne: "This was a common practice at old-fashioned weddings in Wales, among other places. The bride is generally expected to make a great show of resistance to her departure, and to lament loudly." As late as the eighteenth century, a custom that often accompanied weddings in Wales was a race by the male members of the wedding party to the couple's future residence, with food or a silk scarf (originally the bride's garter, a potent love charm) typically awarded to the winner. Benjamin Malkin commented on this contest: "Ill may it befall the traveller, who has the misfortune of meeting a Welsh wedding on the road. He would be inclined to suppose he had fallen

in with a company of lunatics escaped from their confinement." At Scottish country weddings, a related custom, to "ride the brose," involved the groom's attendants racing to the bride's house, with the first to arrive receiving a "cog of brose," or "good fat broth made for the occasion," according to Jamieson. He continued, "The boast of the winner was how far on with the brose he was before the rest of the company arrived."

PIGGESNYE * Term of endearment for one's sweetheart (literally a darling little *pig's eye*) originated by Chaucer, who is also credited with inspiring the tradition of sending love notes on Saint Valentine's Day. In pre-nineteenth-century times, bachelors drew maids' names from a box or hat as their *valentine* for the year. The Church tried to graft a religious holiday onto this long-standing tradition by substituting saints' names for those of the opposite sex, but this attempt proved unpopular and was abandoned in the sixteenth century. The drawing of names was taken somewhat seriously, as we learn from Henry Bournes's 1725 *Antiquities of the Common People:* "It is a ceremony, never omitted among the vulgare, to draw . . . a name, which is called their Valentine, and is also look'd upon as a good omen of their being man and wife afterwards." On Saint Valentine's Day, care was once exercised among the unwed when walking about, as this 1872 excerpt from the periodical *Punch* described:

> The belief is universal . . . that if you are single, the first unmarried person you meet outside the house on St. Valentine's Day will exercise an important influence over your future destiny. Fortunately there is a simple way of evading the hand of Fate, open to those who desire a greater freedom in their choice of a partner in wedlock— at least if they are willing to remain indoors till the expiration of the spell [at noon].

John Gay presented this custom in verse:

> Thee first I spied, and the first swain we see,
> In spite of fortune, shall our true love be.

If an eighteenth-century man was highly infatuated with his valentine, this romantic sometimes wore the name of his beloved printed on a heart-shaped paper pinned to his sleeve, which led to the expression "wearing one's heart on one's sleeve." Similarly inclined women were inclined to wear a charm called a *love-bagge*, or other token near the heart, as found in Pepys's diary: "And here Mrs. T. shewed me my name upon her breast as her valentine, which will cost me twenty shillings." Rituals such as these were influenced by the ancient belief that birds chose their mates on this day, which Herrick ruefully pondered in verse:

> Oft have I heard both Youths and Virgins say
> Birds chuse their Mates, and couple too, this day;
> But by their flight I never can divine
> When I shall couple with my Valentine.

STEWED-PRUNES * Slang term for London brothels where customers "stewed" in hot water, creating prunelike wrinkles in their fingertips. A jar of these laxative fruits, believed to prevent and cure venereal diseases in Elizabethan times, was sometimes displayed on a front windowsill of these establishments, much as a barber's pole advertised haircuts. Skeat observed that prunes were often considered "a favorite dish in brothels," and were frequently used euphemistically in literature, as in *Henry IV* when Falstaff tells Mistress Quickly, "There's no more faith in thee than in a stewed prune." A red cardinal's hat was another sign symbol commonly used to represent the "stews of bankside," and for good reason. From the twelfth to sixteenth centuries, the powerful bishops of Winchester served as landlord and overseer of as many as twenty-two brothels in Southwark, just across the Thames from London. These "courts of frail sisterhood" undoubtedly inspired the line from Shakespeare's *Measure for Measure*, which was performed in the same neighborhood at the Globe Theater: "I have purchased many diseases under this roof." In 1161 Henry II, prompted by a serious outbreak of syphilis, issued an ordinance specifically naming the "Government of the Stewholders in Suthwarke under the Direccion of the Bishoppe of

Winchester." This attempt to reform the stews resulted in weak legislation, such as that brothel keepers "must not receive any nun or man's wife [as employees] without informing the authorities."

Another measure stated that if a man missed the London curfew after dallying too long with the bishop's "Winchester geese," he would be allowed to return to the brothel and claim lodgings. A third provision from the ordinance protected the customer: "No whore must hinder any man but let him come and go as he pleases; if she grabs him by the gown or his hood, she will pay a fine of twenty shillings." William Blake commented upon the foundations of these places in his *Proverbs of Hell:* "Prisons are built with stones of law, brothels with bricks of religion." Henry VIII's short-lived disbanding of the brothels in 1546, after he had contracted venereal disease himself, was memorialized by poet John Taylor:

> The stews in England bore a beastly sway
> Till the eighth Henry banished them away.

Robert Crowley's 1550 *Epigrams*, however, suggested that the disbanding might have had limited benefits:

> The bawds of the stews be turned all out,
> But some think they inhabit all England throughout.

DREAMING-BREAD * Scottish oat-cake specially prepared for a wedding feast from medieval times until the nineteenth century, believed to give virgin maids the power to dream of their future husbands. An 1818 issue of *Edinburgh Magazine* described the ritual necessary for the dream:

> When they reach the bridegroom's door, some cakes of shortbread are broken over the bride's head. It is a peculiar favor to obtain the smallest crumb of this cake . . .

as it possesses the talismanic virtue of favouring such as lay it below their pillow with a nocturnal vision of their future partner for life.

For those not invited to weddings, Saint Agnes's Eve, celebrated on January 20, offered maidens the same opportunity. Until recently, whoever fasted and prayed to this patron saint of virgins and Girl Scouts, and retired without eating her supper, would eagerly expect to dream of the man she was destined to marry. If she was truly serious, in addition to fasting, before retiring she could also "Boil an egg hard, extract the yolk, fill the cavity with salt, and eat the egg, shell and all, then walk backwards to bed." John Keats mentioned this tradition in one of his poems:

> . . . upon St. Agnes' Eve
> Young virgins might have the visions of delight
> If ceremonies due they did aright.

As late as the nineteenth century in Durham, the following rhyme was recited by women to help create this prophetic vision:

> Fair St. Agnes, play thy part,
> And send to me my own sweetheart,
> Not in his best or worst array,
> But in the clothes he wears every day;
> That tomorrow I may him ken,
> From among all other men.

FLITTERWOCHEN * Old English expression meaning "fleeting weeks," the equivalent of what is now referred to as a *honeymoon*, or *lune de miel* in France. In Chaucer's time *flitte* meant "flee or pass away," as often does the initial passion of love. The subsequent term, literally "sweet month," was first used in about 1500, and referred to the inconsistent waxing and waning of the moon but not, at least originally, to a period of one month. The special period after a wedding is an older tradition called *brydlle dayes*, as shown in this excerpt from a 1462 poem, *Wright's Chaste Wife*, about a three-day "home honeymoon":

> He weddyd her fulle sone,
> And ledde her home wyth solemnite,
> And hyld her brydlle dayes three,
> Whan they home come.

A rule of thumb in regard to marriage and money was, according to the eighteenth-century *Statistical Account of Scotland*, "the fuller the moon, the fuller the purse":

> The moon in her increase, full growth, and in her wane, are with them the emblems of a rising, flourishing and declining fortune. At the last period of her revolution, they [the Scots] carefully avoid to engage in any business of importance. . . . The love-sick swain and his nymph [watch] for the coming of the new moon to be noosed together in matrimony. Should the planet happen to be at the height of her splendor when the ceremony is performed, their future life will be a scene of festivity, and all its paths strewed over with rose-buds of delights.

In medieval times, honey was consumed during one's wedding month, often in the form of honey wine, as it was considered an aphrodisiac. Another use of honey, perhaps reserved for honeymoons, was "to know a woman's minde and secrette," as revealed in this excerpt from a sixteenth-century manuscript of a recipe found in Oxford's Bodleian Library:

> Take ye hed of a white pidgeon or of a turtle dove. Burn ye blood and hed to powder. And let it be thorough colde, mingle it wyth quantitie of stone hony. Anoynt ye

brestes of a woman and thou shalle know all her mynd
and what secrettes thou shalt have of her.

In the year 453, Attila the Hun reportedly died of drinking too
much of this honey liquor during his flitterwochen.

AMBERGRIS * Literally "gray amber," a grayish waxy
secretion from the intestines of sperm whales that lubricates
one of its chest bones where it rubs internally. According to
Blount, this substance was written of by Greek authors who

> affirm it to be a kind of bitumen coming forth of the
> fountains or springs in the bottom of the sea, and that
> by floating upon the water it becomes hard . . . The fume
> of it is good against the falling-sickness and comforting
> to the brain.

One of the earliest accounts of ambergris, from 1398, described
it only a little incorrectly as whale sperm, stating that when
dried it "turneth to be substaunce of ambra." Its origin, however, remained a mystery until the nineteenth century. In folk-
lore, this marbled substance often found on the seashore was
proposed to be a "sea mushroom, torn up by tempests." Another theory considered it "bird or fish excrement." Still another imagined it to be a mixture of honey and wax from coastal
honeycombs washed from cliffs. Pliny called it "sunglare," ex-
plaining that it was made of sun rays that hardened upon striking the sea.

Ambergris was used as a brain and nerve tonic, and was
categorized by Herrick with other seventeenth-century body
emollients:

> I sing of Dewes, of Raines, and piece by piece,
> Of Balme, of Oyle, of Spice, and of Amber-Greece.

Ambergris served as an essential ingredient in *amber-cawdle*, reputedly a powerful aphrodisiac and a "fragrant drug," and was used for centuries to make amber perfumes and tinctures. An unlikely perfume-brewing process is outlined in *The Compleat Housewife:* "Take ambergrease and musk, of each an ounce, and put to them a quarter of a pint of spirit of wine; stop it close, tie it down with leather, and set it in horse dung ten or twelve days." Into the nineteenth century, ambergris was consumed as a "cordial" and as an additive to a sweet, spicy wine called *hippocras*, and was used as an ingredient in cooking, especially in sauces. In the early 1600s, Thomas Ravenscroff put ambergris's mystical power as a sexual stimulant into perspective when he wrote,

> You may talk of your amber-cawdles, chocolates and jelly-broths, but they are nothing comparable to youth and beauty; a woman is the only provocative for old age.

FRIBBLER * Eighteenth-century word for a man who expressed profound infatuation with a woman but was unwilling to commit himself to her. *Fribble*, which gave rise to a host of alternate forms, was first recorded as a verb, to trifle, in 1627, and was later used as a noun in the expression "a company of fribbles" in 1664 in John Wilson's comedy, *The Cheats.* Whitford's 1533 *Werke for Householders* alluded to the fribbler:

> The ghostly enemy doth deceyve many persones by the pretence & colour of matrymony in pryvate & secrete contractes. For many men whan they can nat obteyne theyre unclene desyre of the woman, wyll promyse maryage and therupon make a contracte promyse & gyve fayth and trouth eche unto other.... And after that done, they suppose they maye use theyr unclene behav-

your, and somtyme the acte and dede doth folowe, unto
the greate offence of god & their owne soules.

Much Ado About Nothing also mentioned the fribbler:

> Sigh no more ladies, sigh no more,
> Men were deceivers ever,
> One foot in the sea and one on the shore,
> To one thing constant never.

The long-lost word fribbler and its entourage, including the
unlikely nouns *fribbleism* and *fribbledom* (the behavior of a fribbler), was survived only by *frivolous*, which influenced the development of the eighteenth-century noun *frivolity*, and the
nonsense word *fribble-frabble*.

AMOBER * Medieval Welsh legal term for a "maiden fee,"
imposed by the lord of a manor as compensation for forfeiting
his right of *primae noctis*, literally the "first night." Under this
custom, known as *cuillage* in medieval Scotland, he was entitled
to the right of "first refusal" with any woman in his employment on her wedding night. If her husband wished to avoid
this outrageous insult, he was often forced to pay an amober.
Hazlitt wrote that during the late thirteenth-century reign of
Edward I, to add insult to injury, "in Cornwall it was then a
manorial custom . . . that she should find surety to the lord of
the said manor to return to it after the death of her husband,
if he pre-deceased her." Another annoyance faced by newlyweds
was a delay imposed by the Church during medieval times until
their bed was "properly blessed." Francis Blomefield's 1752
History of Norfolk described this custom:

> The pride of the clergy and the bigotry of the laity were
> such that new married couples were made to wait till
> midnight after the marriage day, before they would pro-

nounce a benediction, unless handsomely paid for it, and they durst not undress without it, on pain of excommunication.

HANDFASTING * The custom of a couple shaking hands, as the Romans did over an urn, as a means of sealing a marriage engagement, from the Saxon *handfaestan*. Until the nineteenth century, even *vowing* to wed was considered binding, and the failure to honor this commitment could and did result in legal action for breach of promise. *The Christian State of Matrimony* of 1543 gave some advice: "After the handfastynge and makyng of the contracte, ye churchgoyng and weddyng shuld not be deferred too longe, lest the wickedde sowe hys ungracious sede in the meane season." Brand's *Popular Antiquities* observed that "It was anciently very customary . . . to break a piece of gold or silver in token of a verbal contract of marriage and promises of love; one half whereof was kept by the woman, while the other part remained with the man."

Butler expressed little confidence in the institution of matrimony's ability to help a couple overcome obstacles:

> Marriage, at best, is but a vow,
> Which all men either break or bow;
> Then what will those forbear to do,
> Who perjure when they do but woo?
> Such as beforehand forswear and lie,
> For earnest to their treachery,
> And, rather than a crime confess,
> With greater strive to make it less.

The conceptually similar Scottish "thumb-licking" was an ancient method of sealing an agreement, as described by Jamieson: "In a bargain between two Highlanders, each of them wets the ball of his thumb with his mouth and then joining them together, it is esteemed a very binding act." A *knobstick wedding* was an eighteenth-century English practice akin to the American "shotgun wedding," wherein Church officials called "handfast-makers" forced a man to marry a woman who carried his child.

HEAVERS * On the day after Easter, called "Heaving Monday" in the eighteenth century, groups of men in England and Wales were permitted by custom to physically lift or *heave* women—either in a chair specially adorned for this occasion or in their arms—and require a kiss as a condition of release, as we learn from *The Public Advertiser* of 1787:

> On the first day [Monday], a party of men go with a chair into every house to which they can get admission, force every female to be seated in their vehicle, and lift them three times with loud huzzas; for this they claim the reward of a chaste salute, which those who are too coy to submit to may get an exemption from by a fine of one shilling. On the Tuesday the women claim the same privilege, and pursue their business in the same manner, with this addition—that they guard every avenue to the town, and stop every passenger, pedestrian equestrian or vehicular.

Thomas Pennant, in his 1769 *Tour of Scotland*, added, "In North Wales . . . the young men go about the town and country, from house to house, with a fiddle playing before them, to heave the women." A second London newspaper reported more on the women's offensive:

> The women in general for this period, except those of less scrupulous character, who, for the sake of partaking of a gallon of ale and a plum-cake, which every landlord or

publican is obliged to furnish the revellers with, generally spend the best part of the night in the fields, if the weather is fair, it being strictly according to ancient usage not to partake of the cheer any where else.

This activity, though largely a lower-class pastime, apparently occurred at all levels of society and was said originally to represent Christ's resurrection, but may have had deeper roots in pagan crop fertility rituals.

CURTAIN-LECTURE * Derisive expression, used interchangeably with *curtain-sermon*, during the eighteenth and nineteenth centuries. This scolding, nagging reproof, or "lengthy advice," was issued to a *seeksorrow* husband by his wife after their curtains had been drawn and they were in bed. Chaucer, in *The Wife of Bath's Prologue*, wrote:

> A knowing wife, if she is worth her salt
> Can always prove her husband is at fault.

Douglas Jerrold detailed this *modus operandi* in his 1866 work, *Mrs. Caudle's Curtain Lectures*, regarding the henpecked Job Caudle, who repeatedly sought refuge from his wife's fault-finding. The story unfolds as an episodic monologue of insults and complaints, with each chapter concluded by a brief shrugging comment from Job's pathetic posthumous "diary." A typical bedtime rebuke began like this:

> Well, if a woman hadn't better be in her grave than be married! That is, if she can't be married to a decent man. No, I don't care if you are tired, I shan't let you go to sleep. No, and I won't say what I have to say in the morning; I'll say it now. It's all very well for you to come home at what time you like—it's now half past twelve—

and expect I'm to hold my tongue and let you go to sleep.
What next, I wonder? A woman had better be sold for a
slave at once.

A sixteenth-century proverb seems particularly applicable to
the Caudles: "A deaf husband and a blind wife are always a
happy couple."

Part of a song called *The Curtain Lecture*, written about
1715, allowed the listener to vicariously experience one:

> You filthy beast, you have increased
> My sorrow, grief and care
> By drunkenness. I do confess
> I'm almost in despair.
> For you drink, and sure I think
> You will destroy a woman's joy
> Which I should have, you drunken knave.
> My very heart will rue. . . .
> Take it yourself, you wicked elf.
> I am not bound to wait
> Upon you here. Alas! I fear
> You'll ruin my estate.

John Dryden's works contained this reference to the curtain-
lecture:

> What endless brawls are bred!
> The curtain-lecture makes a mournful bed.

Socrates undoubtedly knew of men who had endured curtain-
lectures, as he advised his students: "By all means marry; if
you get a good woman you'll become happy; if you get a bad
one you'll become a philosopher."

———————

STANGSTER * A husband with marital problems, stem-
ming either from mistreating his wife or being henpecked by

her. The Old English *staeng* came from the Old Norse *stong*, a pole, which this man was forced to sit atop or astride while carried upon the shoulders of a boisterous cavalcade of jeering

neighbors, or represented in effigy and paraded through his village. The 1814 *Costume of Yorkshire* suggested the reason:

> The ancient provincial custom is still occasionally observed in some parts of Yorkshire, though by no means so frequent as it was formerly. It is no doubt intended to expose and ridicule any violent quarrel between man and wife, and more particularly in instances where the pusillanimous husband has suffered himself to be beaten by his virago of a partner.

According to Jamieson's *Scottish Dictionary*, this originally Scandinavian ritual was more severe than it may seem: ". . . a mark of the highest infamy. A person who has been treated [thusly] seldom recovers his honour in the opinion of his neighbors." "Riding the stang" was often accompanied by "rough music"— the beating of pots and pans with tongs and other homemade instruments, sometimes accompanied by bagpipes and the blowing of bulls' horns. The commotion generated by this gathering and its participants appears to have aptly reflected the fourteenth-century proverb, "Empty vessels make the most noise." Ray wrote that this procession was also "used by some colleges in Cambridge to stang scholars in Christmas-time, being to cause them to ride on a colt staff or pole for missing chapel."

Jamieson cited a Scottish account that implied that the stang was not a foolproof form of justice: "When they cannot lay hold of the culprit, they put some young fellow on the stang, who proclaims that it is not on his account that he is thus treated." Remnants of stang-inspired rough music and vigilantism lingered into the twentieth century, as is evident in this vignette from P. D. Ditchfield's 1901 *Old English Customs:* "Friday evening is not considered a correct or suitable time for courtship. The first person spying a couple so engaged enters the house, seizes the frying-pan and beats on it a tattoo." A New Year's Day tradition in England once required any person encountered by a stang procession to "ride the stang" or pay a penalty.

10. Clothes Make the Man
Codde-Pieces, Galligaskins, and Fripperies

CODDE-PIECE * A triangular piece of fabric often decorated and used to mimic the male genitalia (*cod* was once a
common name for a bag and, by extension, the scrotum), which
began innocently enough as a kind of ornamental jockstrap.
From the 1540s until almost the end of the century, this external clothing accessory, known to the French as a boastful-
sounding *braguette*, was sported by the male English aristocracy.
Over time, the padding and animal-bone framework increased
to unbelievable dimensions to give the wearer the coveted appearance of having a permanent erection. Especially toward the
end of its heyday, writers used this embellishment to ridicule
weak or silly individuals. In Shakespeare's *Love's Labour's Lost*,
Berowne scornfully calls himself

> The anointed sovereign of sighs and groans,
> Liege of all loiterers and malcontents,
> Dread prince of plackets [petticoats], king of codpieces.

These curious pronouncements of virility were commonly
donned by royalty, including Henry VIII, who had one for his
suit of armor that was believed to bring fertility to a barren
woman, if she could touch it with a pin. Even Henry's nine-
year-old son, later Edward VI, can be seen in Tudor portraiture
attired in one. This bizarre, multifunctional fashion reached its
height of popularity by the 1560s, being used occasionally to
support a flagpole in marching processions, as a handy pin-
cushion in case a man's garments required adjustment, or as a

toothpick holder. Herrick showcased the codde-piece's potential for use in pilfering dinnerware at banquets:

> When he goes to any publick feast,
> Eats, to one's thinking, of all there the least.
> What saves the master of the house thereby?
> When, if the servants search they may descry,
> In his codde-piece, dining being done,
> Two napkins cram'd up, and a silver spoon.

According to the *Oxford English Dictionary*, by 1577, not to be outdone, women began to wear doublets "with pendant codpeeces on the breast."

FRIPPERY * Seventeenth-century archaism for cast-off garments, as well as an old clothing exchange run by a fripperer, said by Mayhew to be "one of the most ancient of callings." He provided details about the fripperies of London:

> Of Old Clothes Exchanges there are now two, both adjacent, the first one opened by Mr. Isaac being most important. This is 100 feet by 70, and is the mart to which the collectors of the cast-off apparel of the metropolis bring their goods for sale. The goods are sold wholesale and retail, for an old clothes merchant will buy either a single hat or an entire wardrobe or a sackful of shoes—I need not say pairs for odd shoes are not rejected. In one department of "Isaac's Exchange," however, the goods are not sold to parties who buy for their own wearing, but to the old clothes merchant, who buys to sell again. In this portion of the mart are 90 stalls, averaging about six square feet each.

Mayhew also gave a glimpse of the rough and chaotic nature of these places:

The confusion and clamour before the institution of the present arrangements were extreme. Great as was the extent of the business transacted, people wondered how it could be accomplished, for it always appeared to a stranger that there could be no order whatever in all the disorder. The wrangling was incessant, nor were the trade contests always confined to wrangling alone. The passions of the Irish often drove them to resort to cuffs, kicks and blows, which the Jews, although with a better command over their tempers, were not slack in returning.

Frippery might have been influenced by its contemporary, *fripponerie*, French for roguery, and by the mid-nineteenth century, had become synonymous with a showily dressed person. Prayers to Saint Anne, patron saint of fripperers, were believed to increase these shopkeepers' merchandise turnover while preventing theft.

PRICKMEDAINTY * Sixteenth-century man-about-town who coifed himself in an overly careful manner, frequently seek-

ing the services of his barber, and who was, by Jamieson's estimation, "ridiculously exact in dress or carriage." In the

1600s, barbershops were the site of such idleness that legislation was enacted, with specific penalties, to discourage loitering in these places. Musical instruments such as guitars were commonly kept on hand to allow waiting customers to amuse themselves by making *barber's-music*, once estimated by T. Lewis Davies as being "not usually of much excellence." In *Measure for Measure*, Shakespeare ridiculed these laws, which were often posted in the places where they were most likely to be broken:

> Laws for all faults,
> Stand like the forfeits in a barber's shop,
> As much in mock as mark.

Later, satirical replacements were displayed in memory of these older statutes, such as "Rules for Seemly Behavior," collected by Nares in nineteenth-century Yorkshire barbershops:

> Who rudely takes another's turn,
> A forfeit mug [of beer] may manners learn.
> Who reverentless shall swear or curse,
> Must lug seven farthings from his purse.
> Who checks the barber in his tale,
> Must pay for each a pint of ale.
> Who will or cannot miss his hat,
> While trimming, pays a pint for that.
> And he who can or will not pay,
> Shall hence be sent half trimmed away.

Jonathan Swift, in the preface to his *Tale of a Tub*, commented on the dangerous irony of dull humor: "It is with wits as with razors, which are never apt to cut those they are employed on, as when they have lost their edge."

MAY-DEW ✳ Morning droplets of water, gathered usually on the first day of May, believed from medieval times to the

1800s to contain special beauty- and health-enriching properties, which "preserved the face from wrinkles, blotches and the
traces of old age," as in this rhyme:

> Beauty come, freckles go,
> Dewdrops make me white as snow.

A similar pre-nineteenth-century magic elixir, often found in
fairy tales, whose properties were reputed to enhance the
beauty, youthfulness, and even the wealth of the imbiber, was
called *dancing-water*. Noble and peasant alike, including Catherine of Aragon and her entourage, visited the English heath on
May Day to enhance their appearance through one of nature's

liquid miracles. E. M. Wright explained May-dew's perennial
popularity: "To wash in May-dew was supposed to strengthen
the joints and muscles, the reason given being that the dew
had in it all the 'nature' of the spring herbs and grasses, and
therefore it must be wonderfully strengthening." Hone's 1827
Every-Day Book acquainted the reader with some of the partic-
ulars of dew-gathering in Edinburgh:

> About four o'clock in the morning there is an unusual
> stir . . . a hurrying of gay throngs of both sexes through

the King's park to Arthur's seat. In the course of half an
hour the entire hill is a moving mass of all sorts and sizes.

Directions for making an eighteenth-century facial mudpack—
also intended "to take off freckles"—included the following
steps:

> Take either bean flower water, elder-flower water or May-
> dew gathered from corn, four spoonfuls, and add to it one
> spoonful of oil of tartar per deliquium; mix it well to-
> gether and often wash the face with it; let it dry on.

In 1850, Launceston recorded the following Cornish remedy:

> They say that a child who is weak in the back may be
> cured by drawing him over the grass wet with morning
> dew. The experiment must be thrice performed, that is
> on the mornings of the 1st, 2nd and 3rd of May.

Well into the nineteenth century, birth records indicate that
January was the month when most babies were born in England. Historians speculate that this phenomenon was due to
the increased incidence of sexual activity in the spring, reaching
a peak in the "lusty month of May."

GORGAYSE * Middle English word which meant "ele-
gant, fashionable." Its roots were in the Latin *gurges*, used in
the third century to refer to the throat, via the French *gargale*,
the windpipe. From this same root came the medieval *gorget*,
a large flat piece of precious metal such as gold, beaten thin
and worn about the neck and breast as a custom-fitted disk.

In the fifteenth century, a new style of women's headdress
was devised; dubbed a *gorgias*, it also covered the throat. It
partially replaced the long-popular *wimple*, which covered the
head as well and is now worn only by nuns. This fashion was

apparently so admired that gorgayse became an adjective for "tastefulness in dress," from which the derivative, *gorgeous*, has survived into modern times.

Dr. Andry's *Orthopædia* provided a less than definitive picture of the ideal neck:

> The neck is commonly looked upon as part of the chest. . . . The neck, to be well-shaped, must be round, and moderately long and slender, but at the same time it must have a sort of plumpness or fullness, so that the Pomum Adami [Adam's Apple] may not appear, especially in women.

The *Shepherd's Prognostication* presented valuable tips to readers on evaluating people's psychological attributes, based upon their necks:

> The neck short signifieth one to be witty; such as are strong about the knot or joint of the neck are of good capacity; such as are weak, are dullards. The neck big, to be strong; big and fleshy, to be ireful; the neck long and small, signifieth to be fearful.

BUCKRAM * A high-quality cotton/linen fabric stiffened with glue, rumored to have originated among the Tartars in Bukhara, a fabled city of Central Asia. Entering the English language before the fifteenth century, possibly from the Latin *buchiranus*, "goatskin," buckram was sometimes used figuratively to indicate a "starched pomposity," said to have been particularly found in the lowest echelon of attorneys. Because of buckram's stiff nature but light weight, it is still employed to provide firm internal shape to garments, hats, and drapery, after an earlier, seventeenth-century use by women to augment their bust size, which Herrick derided in *No Fault in Women:*

No fault in women, to make show
Of largeness, when th'are nothing so;
When true it is, the out-side swells
With inward Buckram, little else.

Lawyers were derisively termed *buckram bags*, and later *green bags*, as they were commonly seen carrying early briefcases made of green buckram, often fashionably hung from their belts. The earliest recorded usage of buckram, in 1589, referred to "buckram Bishops of Italy" who were said to be "inclined to arrogance." Buckram was also used as a verb, meaning "to give the false appearance of strength."

HOBNAIL * Seventeenth-century nickname for a farmer or *ploughman* whose shoes were frequently repaired with large-headed nails or *hobnails*, and patched or tipped with pieces of metal. A more appropriate choice of nail for shoe repairs at that time was a *sparable*, which was headless and wedge-shaped, like the sparrow's bill that inspired its creation. Shoemakers were, in some locales, thought to be able to divine people's futures based on the wear of their shoes, as we see in this nineteenth-century Suffolk rhyme:

Tip at the toe, live to see woe;
Wear at the side, live to be bride;
Wear at the ball, live to spend all;
Wear at the heel, live to save a deal.

Workmen's shoes were usually not made in left and right versions until the 1800s. Even so, a shoe was to be put on the right foot first, as in this verse from *Hudibras:*

Augustus having b' oversight
Put on his left shoe 'fore his right

> Had like to have been slain that day,
> By soldiers mutin'yng for pay.

A host of omens, both fortunate and inauspicious, involved shoe-related activities, including the throwing of shoes at anyone who was embarking on an important venture, as sixteenth-century poetry from John Heywood illustrates:

> I will streight weie anker and hoyst up sayle,
> And thitherward have me in haste lyke a snayle,
> And home agayne hitherward quicke as a bee,
> Now for good luck, caste an olde shoe after mee.

This is still observed in the tying of shoes or empty cans to the bumper of a newlywed couple's car.

———————

GALLIGASKIN * Baggy trousers of the seventeenth and eighteenth centuries, "a sort of loose long breeches mostly worn by persons on shipboard," according to the *Midshipman's British Mariner's Vocabulary* of 1801. Early trousers were also known as *galley-skins* and *galley-slops*, with reference to sailing vessels and their food preparation areas called *galleys*. In the early 1800s, Noah Webster erroneously summarized the origin of these articles, speculating that "Trowsers were first worn by Gallic Gascons, the inhabitants of Gascony." Galligaskin was a fanciful corruption of the French *greguesques*, meaning "Greekish," hinting at their place of origin, although Cotgrave defined the galligaskin as "A fashion of straight Venetians without codpeeces."

The French have long set fashion trends, as these lines from *Hudibras* confirm:

> And as the French, we conquer'd once,
> Now give us laws for pantaloons,
> The length of breeches, and the gathers,
> Port-cannons, perriwigs and feathers.

This piece of clothing was not always spoken of directly in polite conversation. The first recorded euphemistic substitute for trousers was the term *inexpressibles* in 1790, which later suited Victorian taste so well that a rash of synonyms appeared in the 1830s and 1840s, including *unmentionables, indescribables, innominables, inexplicables, unutterables,* and the superlative *unwhisperables*. About this time, Mark Twain wrote: "Modesty antedates clothes and will be resumed when clothes are no more." The modern word *trousers* was derived from the ancient Celtic word *trews*, or *trooze*, which according to Ware's *Antiquities of Ireland* were "Breeches [that] have hose and stockings sewed together," while the Romans used a Latin word for a similar garment, *laxus*, which became slacks. Pants came from the Italian *pantaleone*.

ISABELLINE * An adjective indicating a grayish-yellow or parchment color, employed until the late nineteenth century. In the first decade of the 1600s, its root word, *isabella*, was first used in an inventory of Queen Elizabeth's wardrobe: "Item, one rounde gowne of Isabella-colour satten . . . set with silver spangles." The only available explanation, though a controversial one, of this word's origin is from Littré's 1863 French dictionary. He suggests that the name for this color was borrowed from Archduchess Isabella of Austria. It seems that at the conclusion of the sixteenth century, she solemnly vowed not to change her *small-clothes*, or underwear, until the town of Ostend, which was under siege by her father, Philip II, was taken. To her dismay, and that of her close friends, this battle continued for another three years. A sixteenth-century equivalent of this practice among men was vowing not to shave or trim one's beard until a particular event took place. In the seventeenth-century poem, *The Cobbler and Vicar of Bray*, we read:

This worthy knight was one that swore
He would not cut his beard,
Till this ungodly nation was
From kings and bishops clear'd.
Which holy vow he firmly kept,
And most devoutly wore
A grisly meteor on his face,
Till they were both no more.

––––––––––

LAVENDYRE * A fourteenth-century woman, or occasionally a man, who laundered clothes, derived from the Latin *lavandaria*, meaning "laundry in need of washing," and Old French *lavandiere*, a laundress. From the fourteenth to sixteenth centuries, a *lavendry* was a place, usually outdoors, where clothing and bedding were washed as carefully as possible, in view of a superstition found in Addy's 1895 *Household Tales:* "If you splash yourself . . . when you wash clothes, you will have a drunken husband." Lavendyre and the modern laundry were influenced by the French and Middle English *laund*, a lawn, pasture, or glade in which recently washed clothes were laid out to dry. The herb name *lavender* is closely related to the modern word laundry, as pungent sprigs of the former were used for perfuming freshly washed and dried linen and preventing mold. Hence, the old expression "to lay up in lavender" meant, by extension, to put something away safely until needed. Skeat verified this in his *Etymological Dictionary*, but added:

> The plant was often laid with fresh-washed linen, and thus came to be associated with the Latin lauare, to wash. But the early form, livendula, tends rather to associate it with liuere, to be livid [blue], from its bluish colour.

Lavender, once an emblem for affection, was worn in the lining of a hat "for all the griefs and pains of the head," giddiness, or "turning of the brain." Culpepper wrote of another use of lavender:

> Two spoonfuls of the distilled water of the flowers taken, helps them that have lost their voice, as also the tremblings and passions of the heart, and faintings and swooning, not only being drank, but applied to the temples, or nostrils to be smelled unto.

For a time, the term "laundering" could apply to the grooming of beards, which were sometimes perfumed, even among the

burliest of men, with lavender tinctures. In this regard, Butler's *Hudibras* referred to whiskers that were "prun'd, and starch'd, and lander'd."

11. *The Ocean Blue*

Grog-Blossoms, Loblollies, and Purl-Men

FUROLE * Glowing electrical fireball, also known as Saint Elmo's fire, or *corposant* (literally "saint's body"), often seen by sailors at the top of a ship's mast, the end of a yardarm, or on a bowsprit before or during a storm. These "little meteors," believed to forewarn of a storm, were often considered to be a sign that the ship enjoyed divine protection, as suggested in William Dampier's 1697 *A New Voyage Round the World:*

> After four o'clock, the thunder and the rain abated, and then we saw a Corpus Sant at our main-top-mast head. This sight rejoic'd our men . . . for the height of the storm is commonly over when the Corpus Sant is seen aloft.

Saint Elmo's name was invoked for deliverance from seasickness and shipwreck, as an angel allegedly had ferried him across the Mediterranean in the third century to save him from persecution. Bailey's dictionary defined this curious apparition:

> [of feu, fire, and *rouler*, to roll, French] A little blaze of fire, appearing by night on the tops of soldiers' lances or at sea on sail-yards, which whirls and leaps in a moment from place to place. . . . If there be two, it is called Castor and Pollux, and is supposed to portend safety, but if but one, it is called Helena, and is thought to forebode shipwreck.

In Shakespeare's *The Tempest*, Ariel turned himself into a furole in order to cause a shipwreck. In this passage the sprite boasts of his mischief:

I boarded the king's ship. . . .
I flamed amazement; sometime I'd divide
And burn in many places; on the topmast,
The yards, and boresprit would I flame distinctly,
Then meet and join Jove's lightnings.

In *Moby Dick*, Melville drew an eerie portrait of the transient furole, along with a clue as to its origin:

"Look aloft!" cried Starbuck. "The corpusants! The corpusants!" All the yard-arms were tipped with a pallid fire; and touched at each tri-pointed lightning-rod-end with three tapering white flames; each of the three tall masts was silently burning in that sulfurous air, like three gigantic wax tapers before an altar.

Long after the dawn of the Age of Electricity, this luminous apparition was given a place in Richard Henry Dana's 1842 classic, *Two Years Before the Mast*, and Smyth's 1867 *Sailor's Word-book*, and was perceived by seamen at least into the late 1880s.

CALENTURE * Bizarre physical and psychological condition, which combined a fever with "a passionate desire to act upon one's hallucinations." Calenture was believed to be caused by the *callidity* or heat of the sun, and derived from the Latin *calor*, heat. It was experienced by sailors in tropical latitudes, who deliriously envisioned the surrounding waters as fields of greenery, and often felt a compulsion to jump overboard, as these lines from Jonathan Swift illustrate:

So by a callenture misled,
The mariner with rapture sees,
On the smooth ocean's azure bed,
Enamelled fields and verdant trees.

Referenced in literature since the late 1500s, calenture also developed a metaphorical sense of zealotry and passion, as in John Donne's obscure adage converse to "ignorance is bliss": "Knowledge kindles calenture in some." Robinson Crusoe, who suffered this ailment early in the classic novel by Daniel Defoe, lamented: "Yet even in this voyage, I had my misfortunes too; particularly, that I was continually sick, being thrown into a violent calenture by the excessive heat of the climate." Fevers that accompanied calentures were long treated with invocations to Saint Hugh of Cluny and other Christian saints, but when these appeals went unheeded, imaginative remedies were tried, such as one found in *Rustic Speech and Folk-Lore:*

> Take wood-lice, the species which roll up on being touched, and swallow them as pills; wrap a spider up in a cobweb and swallow it like a pill; place a spider in a nutshell and suspend it around the neck in a small bag; take the eare of a mouse and bruise it, then take salte and stamp them together and make a pultas with vinegar, and so lay it to the wrists; write this charm on a three-cornered piece of paper, and wear it round the neck till it [presumably the paper] drops off: "Ague, ague, I thee defy, Three days shiver, Three days shake, Make me well for Jesus' sake."

"Dr. Hall's Plaister for an Ague" was an eighteenth-century preventative measure against fever:

> Take a pennyworth of black soap, one pennyworth of gunpowder, one ounce of tobacco snuff, and a glass of brandy; mix these in a mortar very well together. Spread plaisters on leather for the wrists, and lay them on an hour before you expect the fit.

Butler once commented upon the appearance of sick and calentured people, "How holy people look when they are seasick."

LOBLOLLY * A type of hearty gruel commonly served to sailors. Robert Leslie's *Old Sea Wings, Ways and Words* pointed out that loblolly was a nineteenth-century "name for the seafaring dish of porridge, sometimes called burgoo," and later, oral medicines in general, frequently prescribed to shipboard patients in the absence of more potent preparations. Loblolly's name was borrowed from the slurping sound made by someone consuming this "spoon-meat," as it was sometimes called. Loblolly, whose virtues were discussed as early as 1597 in Gerarde's *Herbal*, was related to *lobscouse*, a meat and vegetable stew, because of its *lob*, or hot, bubbly nature, and by being found in a ship's mess hall. Loblolly was described by Admiral Smyth's *Sailor's Word-book* as "one of the oldest and most savory of the regular forecastle dishes."

In the eighteenth century, *loblolly-doctor* became a derisive nautical appellation for a ship's doctor or surgeon, whose ablebodied assistant during surgical procedures was given the telltale name *understrapper*. One of these helpers, whom Tobias Smollett wrote of in his 1748 novel, *Roderick Ransom*, lamented:

> I was not altogether without mortifications, which I not only suffered from the rude insults of the sailors and petty officers, among whom I was known as Loblolly Boy, but also from the disposition of Morgan.

Ambrose Bierce offered a practical recommendation for anyone who was considering doing business with a knife-wielding loblolly-doctor: "Before undergoing a surgical operation, arrange your temporal affairs—you might live."

ROUND-ROBIN * Eighteenth-century term of nautical origin, derived from the French *ruban*, literally a "round ribbon." It referred to the clever format of a document presented to the captain of a British naval vessel or other authority, which listed grievances in a manner described by Dr. Johnson's dictionary: "A written petition of remonstrance, signed by several persons round a ring or circle." The signatures appeared in a radiating fashion, like the spokes of a wheel. This arrangement gave little clue as to the identity of the first signatory, who might have otherwise been singled out for punishment—which could well have been execution by hanging.

As late as 1881, Davies's *Supplemental English Glossary* defined round-robin as: "A seditious person, perhaps because dissatisfied people sometimes make a complaint to their superiors by a round-robin." Round-robins, whether drawn up at sea or on land, were generally of limited scale, allowing for perhaps two dozen signatories at most, but could apparently accommodate multitudes, if this 1755 remark of Lord Chesterfield can be believed: "If I thought it could be of any use, I could easily present them with a round robin to that effect of above a thousand . . . names." A shipboard agitator, who might have been the catalyst in initiating such actions, was sometimes called a *sea lawyer*.

GROG-BLOSSOM * Eighteenth-century expression for the red nose of a drunkard caused by dilation of blood vessels in long-term alcohol consumption. Despite its ironic current usage as potent liquor, *grog* originally referred to rum diluted with an equal part of water, rather than served straight as was customary. This "water-bewitched" (watered down) drink was abruptly substituted for the straight by the inflexible and unpopular admiral Edward Vernon in August 1740, and issued to his naval crew in an attempt to reduce on-board intoxication.

Grog was coined as a result of Admiral Vernon's derisive nickname, "Old Grog," from his oft-worn cloak (or *breeches*, said Skeat) made from *grogram*, a coarse-textured fabric of wool mixed with silk and mohair, and used as a verb since the 1870s. By the mid-1800s, a *groggery* had come to mean a sleazy drinking establishment, especially one that catered to sailors. Thomas Trotter composed this satirical verse in 1781 illustrating Vernon's deed:

> A mighty bowl on deck he drew,
> And filled it to the brink;
> Such drank the Burford's gallant crew,

And such the gods shall drink;
The sacred robe which Vernon wore
Was drenched within the same,
And hence his virtues guard our shore,
And grog derives its name.

Winston Churchill had a surprisingly low opinion of the Royal Navy: "Don't talk to me about naval tradition. It's nothing but rum, sodomy and the lash."

Grog appears to have been borrowed by the French for *grognard*, an aged soldier of Napoleon's Old Guard, who enjoyed spinning yarns about his war experiences.

PRESS-GANG * Party of sailors who roamed the streets of seventeenth- to nineteenth-century seaports, often at night, in search of "recruits" for immediate sea duty. They were sometimes assisted by a *crimper*, a saloon keeper paid for selecting candidates for kidnapping, as well as serving drugged liquor to his unsuspecting patrons. A "runner" finished off the subdued victims (whose duty pay, ironically, was withheld to pay the crimper's fee) by dragging them back to the ship. Dr. Johnson once gave his sardonic opinion of enlisting in the Royal Navy:

> No man will be a sailor who has the contrivance enough to get himself into a jail, for being in a ship is being in jail, with the chance of being drowned. . . . A man in jail has more room, better food and commonly better company.

This relatively modern use of the term "press" is a descendant of a much older English tradition, dating from medieval times and lasting into the eighteenth century. During that period, earnest-money or *press-money* was an advance often paid to various types of recruits, which served as legal proof of their enlistment. The money was not always forthcoming, as Pepys's August 22, 1667, diary entry indicates:

> I went to examine some men that are put in [a holding area] for rescuing of men that were pressed into service, and we do plainly see that the desperate condition that we put men into for want of their pay makes them mad, they being as good men as ever were in the world, and would readily serve the king again were they but paid. Two men lept overboard, among others, into the Thames out of the vessel into which they were pressed, and were shot by soldiers placed there to keep them; so much people do to avoid the king's service!

The expression "pressed into service" had a variety of applications beyond the dockyards. Prisoners, for example, could be released early if they "volunteered" to perform unpleasant tasks, often in the army. Because of the brutal conditions in the Royal Navy and the subsequent high desertion rate of crew members, these seventeenth- and eighteenth-century recruitment practices were necessary and common, and "impressment" was even practiced in houses of worship, as revealed in a 1739 journal entry of Methodist minister John Wesley: "In the middle of the sermon, the press-gang came and seized one of the hearers."

PURL-MEN * A peculiar class of itinerant eighteenth- and nineteenth-century beer-sellers, who plied their trade on the Thames and other navigable waterways of southern England. Their name is borrowed from an ancient and obsolete practice called *purling*, which infused wormwood, a flavoring agent, into the ales they sold. This ale was designated by them as *purl*, though Mayhew added this footnote: "There is not one

of them with whom I have conversed that has the remotest idea of the meaning of it." Mayhew introduced a purl-man to his readers:

> There is one of these river spirit-sellers who has pursued the avocation for the greater part of his life; he is a native of the south of Ireland, now very old, and a little, shrivelled-up man. He may still be seen every day, going from ship to ship by scrambling over the quarters where they are lashed together in tiers—a feat sometimes attended with danger to the young and strong; yet he works his way with the agility of a man of twenty, gets on board the ship he wants, and when there, were he not so well known, he might be thought to be some official sent to take an inventory of the contents of the ship, for he has at all times an ink-bottle hanging from one of his coat buttons, a pen stuck over his ear, spectacles on his nose, a book in his hand, and really has all the appearance of a man determined on doing business of some sort or other.

Traveling in small rowboats, these men often did a brisk business, developing a clientele that allowed them, under the best of circumstances, to buy a public-house after as few as four to five years and, said Mayhew, "become men of substance." Since the eighteenth century, however, beer acquired from local breweries, heated to near boiling and flavored with gin, sugar, and ginger, has generally been drunk in lieu of home-made purl.

SCUTTLED-BUTT * This nautical equivalent of the office water cooler served as the hub of informal conversation aboard English ships of the eighteenth and nineteenth centuries. At that time, a *butt* was a hogshead or barrel "of 104–140 gallon capacity" whose name was adopted from the fifteenth-century French *botte*. A square hole large enough to allow water to be scooped out in a cup was cut or "scuttled" (as in wrecking or "scuttling" a ship by cutting "scuttles" in it) into the upper part of this reservoir. Phillips's 1706 dictionary makes mention of scuttles as "square holes, capable for the body of a man to pass through at any hatch-way or part of the deck, into any room below; also those little windows and long holes which are cut out in cabins to let in light." The direct linguistic descendant of the scuttled-butt, *scuttlebutt*, acquired its name from its proximity to the on-board "grapevine," and has since become synonymous with gossip on land and sea.

HORSE-LATITUDES * A band of light winds and calm seas adjacent to the northern and southern edges of the trade winds, from 30° to 35° north and south latitudes. The often becalmed or unpredictable northern region could significantly lengthen voyages to the New World from Europe. George Forster's 1777 *Voyage Round the World* suggested a reason for the odd name: "The latitudes where these calms chiefly reign are named the horse-latitudes by mariners . . . because they are fa-

tal to horses and other cattle which are transported to . . .
[America]." The horse-latitudes might have been so named because of the large quantities of water horses consumed, leading
to their "fatalities," as they were sometimes slaughtered there
because of shipboard water shortages. In *Elementary Meteorology*,
Robert Scott, who apparently never made the crossing himself,
gave a spurious etymology for horse-latitudes, claiming they
originated "from the Spanish El Golfo de las Yegnas, the Mares'
Sea, from its unruly and boisterous nature . . . in contradistinc-
tion to the Trade-wind zone, so called from the pleasant

weather to be met with there." The horse-latitudes' realm of
relentless tranquility gave rise to a second nautical appellation,
the nineteenth-century "doldrums," a well-known Latinesque
psychological slang term related to *dold*, a Scottish word for
dull or stupid. Though not synonymous with "horse-latitudes,"
the doldrums came to indicate less specific regions where the
trade winds offset one another resulting in light winds.

12. The Sacred and Profane
Dog-Floggers, Adamites, and Sockdolagers

BYTESHEIP * Mocking expression for a bishop, intended as a play upon his official title, likening him to a shepherd who bit the animals he was charged with protecting. Beaumont and

Fletcher used a derivative of bytesheip in their early seventeenth-century play *Rule of a Wife:*

> How like a sheep-biting rogue,
> Taken in the manner,
> And ready for the halter,
> Dost thou now look.

Sixteenth-century poet Robert Semple made this allusion:

> They halde it still up for a mocke,
> How Maister Patrick fedd his flock;
> Then to the count this crafty loun [rogue]
> To a bytescheip made him boun [ready].

Shakespeare used a variation of bytesheip, *sheep-biter*, in *Twelfth Night*, and in *Measure for Measure* he wrote, "Show your sheep-biting face and be hanged [in] an hour."

The often unpopular bishop was sometimes mocked when milk, pottage, or soup was burned, in the common phrases, "the milk was *bishopped*" and "the bishop's foot was in it." Francis Grose suggested a possible origin for these expressions: "When a bishop in former times passed through a village, everyone ran out to receive his blessing, and during their absence the milk was burned." In the 1500s, someone referred to as "the bishop's son" had considerable political influence. In the 1830s, bishop was also employed colloquially as a sinister verb meaning "to murder by drowning," after a bishop reportedly drowned a boy in order to sell his body for dissection.

GODZIP ✳ Old English term for a godparent who answered for a child during baptismal ceremonies. These elders enjoyed the privileged status, once called a *godsib*, which allowed them to discuss the well-being and affairs of their godchildren, based

on a benevolent maternal affection called *storge*. Jamieson commented on the godzip's surprisingly dominant relationship to the child: "In consequence of the spiritual relation supposed to be constituted at baptism . . . the sponsor was viewed as equal to that of the natural parent." Godparents once were not allowed to be married to each other, however, reflecting an old proverb and self-fulfilling prophecy: "First at the font, never at the altar," as we learn from Brand's *Popular Antiquities:* "It is ominous for a couple attached to each other, or engaged, to stand together for the same child; if they do, it is apprehended something will happen to prevent their marrying together." Over time, these terms, as well as the sacred institution they represented, declined in importance, as gossip was transformed into a term for a friend with whom entertaining trivia were exchanged. Thomas Shipman wrote in 1666 of the corresponding decrease in godzips' generosity at baptismal gatherings, or "gossipings," where at one time they had routinely brought gifts of gilt silver in various forms:

> Especially since gossips now
> Eat more at christenings than bestow;
> Formerly when they us'd to troul [give]
> Gilt bowls of sack, they gave the bowl.
> Two spoons at least, an ill use kept;
> 'Tis well now if our own be left.

By the late 1600s, *godsib* had established itself as the more generalized noun (and later verb) *gossip*, a *thrunk-wife* or "busybody" who spoke idly of others in their absence.

SOCKDOLAGER * Early nineteenth-century term for a climax or crescendo, which in salesmanship might be called the "close" or "finisher." Sockdolager was constructed from *sock*, a knockout punch, and *doxology*, a motivational hymn or "verse of thanksgiving" sung near the conclusion of church services. Sermons were once so carefully prepared to maximize the dramatic impact of the sockdolager that clever preachers sometimes noted in the margins where they "cough'd or hemm'd," as Butler alluded to in *Hudibras:*

> And with hearty noise he spoke 'em
> The ignorant for current took 'em . . .
> And when he happened to break off
> In the middle of his speech or cough,
> H' had hard words ready to show why
> And tell what rules he did it by. . . .
> Have pow'rful preachers plied their tongues,
> And laid themselves out, and their lungs;
> Us'd all means, both direct and sinister,
> I' th' power of gospel-preaching minister?

Sockdolager became a popular word in America for an unexpected event, particularly a violent one. In Davy Crockett's 1835 account of his American wilderness exploration, *Bear Hunt*, he recalled giving a "fellow a socdolager over the head with the barrel of my gun." In *Huckleberry Finn*, Mark Twain wrote: "The thunder would go rumbling and grumbling away, and quit—and then rip comes another flash and another sockdolager." By extension, sockdolager denoted surprise ensnarement by a patented double-pronged fishhook of the 1840s, which upon being bitten snapped together in a fish's mouth.

BOWSSEN * Common medieval practice, based upon Celtic well worship, which survived at least into the seventeenth century. Bowssening addressed mental illness by a form of exorcism, using a "holy well," of which there were many in the British Isles. Bowssen was related to the ancient Cornish word *beuzi*, "to drown." Borlase, in his 1758 *Natural History of Cornwall*, highlighted this procedure:

> A very singular manner of curing madness in the Parish
> of Altarnun was to place the disordered in mind on the

brink of a square pool filled with water from St. Nun's
Well. The patient, having no intimation of what was intended, was, by a sudden blow on the breast, tumbled
into the pool, where he was tossed up and down by some
persons of superior strength, till, being quite debilitated,
his fury forsook him; he was then carried to Church, and
certain masses sung over him.

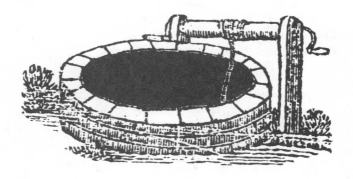

Carew, in his *Survey of Cornwall*, described a wall where

> the frantick person set, and from thence tumbled head-
> long into the pond, where a strong fellow tossed him up
> and down, until the patient, by foregoing his strength,
> had somewhat forgot his fury. If there appeared small
> amendment, he was bowssened again and again.

John Fletcher's 1610 *Faithfull Shepherdesse* reported that the holy
well also functioned as a "fountain of youth":

> For to that holy wood is consecrate
> A virtuous well, about whose flowery banks
> The nimble-footed fairies dance their rounds
> By pale moonshine, dipping oftentimes
> Their stolen children, so to make them free
> From dying flesh and dull mortality.

In his 1631 *Tom of All Trades*, Thomas Powell cynically advised how to create a holy well:

> Let them finde out some strange water, some unheard of spring. It is an easie matter to discolour or alter the taste of it in some measure. Report strange cures that it hath done. Beget a superstitious opinion of it. Good fellowship shall uphold it, and the neighboring townes shall all sweare for it.

Recently, scientific investigation has shown some of these wells to contain relatively high concentrations of lithium salts, which are now sometimes used by psychiatrists to calm hyperactive patients.

———

PEWAGE * An annual rent paid to a church for a pew space occupied by a single sitter, called a *bottom-room* in Scotland from the seventeenth to nineteenth centuries. Pewage's root word, *pew*, can be traced to the Latin *podium* via Old French *puye*, a raised platform like the balconies where Roman emperors and dignitaries witnessed performances and gruesome spectacles. Pews were introduced into churches in the late 1400s, and by 1520, a *pew-fellow* had become a fellow worshipper as well as a companion in general. A verb form of pewage developed in the 1600s that was used derisively to mean "confined," as reflected in this account from 1831 regarding "men who were as willingly pewed in the parish church as their sheep were in night folds." A particular type of pew, called a *parlor-pew* or *squire's-pew*, was a chamber sometimes found in rural English churches that was comfortably furnished much like a parlor. In the 1700s and 1800s, when many people rented their pews, these rooms were available for wealthy patrons such as the lord of a manor or the squire of his household, much as "luxury boxes" are available today at sports stadiums. An account in London's *Daily News* of 1896 scornfully reported on "the village church, lately in possession of a squire's-pew, carpeted, with fireplace, chairs and tables, a snuggery wherein the great man snored unobserved."

In the seventeenth century, an iron-framed hourglass was sometimes placed conspicuously on or near the pulpit; its sands ran out in one hour, then considered the legitimate length of a sermon. This device was featured in a story related by Henry Bohn:

> A tedious spin-text, having tired out his congregation by a sermon which lasted through one turn of his glass and three parts of the second, without any prospect of its coming to a close, was, out of compassion to the yawning auditory, greeted with this short hint by the sexton, "Pray sir, be pleased, when you have done, to leave the key under the door," and thereupon departing, the congregation followed him.

Jonathan Swift, who may have attended just such a service, wrote in *A Sermon on Sleeping in Church*, "Opium is not so stupefying to many persons as an afternoon sermon."

LENTEN-FACED * Adjective for a dejected, emaciated, mournful-looking sixteenth-century fellow who had recently undergone the trials of fasting. Not surprisingly, the Scottish term *lentfull* meant a melancholy disposition, while the Latin-based French adverbs *lente* and *lentement* meant "slowly or sluggishly," as the six-week lenten period must have passed for many. In this spirit of asceticism, a *lenten suit* became one of homely style and fabric, probably well worn. Nares commented that in the same way, a "lenten pye" denoted a pie made with a "stale hare," no doubt an apt description of "the fare of old times in Lent." Because of the abstinence implied, a *lenten-lover* denoted a bashful wooer hesitant to touch his mistress. Rabelais characterized such people as "Those who approach love as contemplative, who never meddle with the flesh." Old proverbs, such as one preserved by John Ray, even cautioned against lenten marriages: "Marry in Lent, live to repent."

Though frowned upon by the Church for parishioners' tables, geese were sometimes consumed by the twelfth-century clergy on days when meat was prohibited, including the forty days of Lent. The Church reasoned that, as a result of their having germinated from barnacles (see *Barnacle-Goose*, page 1), they were more fish than meat, according to Giraldus Cambrensis:

> They do not breed and lay eggs like other birds, nor do they ever hatch any eggs . . . Hence bishops and religious men in some parts of Ireland . . . dine off these birds at the time of fasting, because they are not flesh nor born of flesh.

The porpoise was long considered a tasty fish, and could be eaten during Lent. However, its later reclassification as meat prompted melancholy in at least one nineteenth-century letter writer: "It is lamentable to think how much sin [porpoises] thus occasioned among our forefathers, before they were discovered to be mammalian."

FULLUHT * Anglo-Saxon expression for the Christian ceremony of baptism, used until the thirteenth century. As is common whenever a religious idea is superimposed upon an existing tradition, an odd variation of this sacrament occurred, called in this case *head-washing*, which E. M. Wright characterized as "not so much a feast as a free drinking." This dialectic term for toasting and drinking to the health of a new baby was also called "wetting the baby's head" and reflected the ancient custom in the British Isles of pouring ale over a newborn's head. The Church fostered hair-raising tales to encourage baptism, such as this one from *The Discovery of Witchcraft:*

> The devil teacheth witches to make ointments of the bowels and members of children, whereby they ride in the air and accomplish all their desires. So as, if there be any children unbaptized, or not guarded with the sign of the cross or orisons, then the witches may and do catch them from their mother's sides at night, or out of their cradles . . . and after burial, steal them out of graves and seethe them in a cauldron, until their flesh be made potable.

Baptism was considered the ultimate safeguard against an infant being switched by fairies or night-hags with one of their runts, or "changelings." John Strypes's 1567 *Annals of the Reformation* related that midwives took an oath not to "suffer any other bodies child to be set, brought or laid before any woman delivered of child or in place of her natural child . . . nor any kind

of sorcery or incantation in the time of travail of any woman."
Spencer elaborated on this "exchange" in his *Fairy Queen:*

> From thence a fairy thee unweeting reft
> There as though slep'st in tender swadling band,
> And her base elfin brood there for thee left,
> Such men do changelings call, so chang'd by fairy theft.

Pennant's *Tour of Scotland* turned up glimpses of lost souls, "little spectres called *tarans,* or souls of unbaptised infants, [who] were often seen flitting among the woods and secret places, bewailing in their soft voices their hard fate." Until well into the nineteenth century, headless *heath-hounds* of Devonshire folklore were believed to be animated by the spirits of children who had died without receiving baptism. Devonshire legend sets forth that these ill-fated creatures, like tarans, would "ramble among the woods at night, making wailing noises." Baptism could even protect children from the pernicious influence of the moon, as is found in *Lancashire Legends:* "Should children observe the moon looking into their rooms, they are taught to avert her influence by repeating, 'I see the moon, the moon sees me. God bless the priest that christened me.' " Until the last century in northern England, any mortal stepping on the grave of an unbaptized child ran the risk of contracting a fatal disease known as "grave-scab." Witches, however, possessed a natural immunity to this malady and were often on the lookout for the unbaptized in churchyards, as this anonymous couplet suggested:

> At midnight hours o'er the kirk-yard she raves,
> And howks unchristen'd weans out of their graves.

Private baptism was not considered as legitimate as baptism in a church, and therefore a privately christened child was said to have been "half-baptized." In Yorkshire, if a boy and girl were baptized together, the boy was baptized first or risked growing up with feminine, and the girl with masculine, facial characteristics.

ADAMITISM * In the eighteenth and nineteenth centuries, adamitism meant "nakedness for religious reasons," and referred to the dress code for *Adamites*, members of several sects from as long ago as the second century and as recently as the early 1600s, who preferred to dress like Adam and Eve. Dyche attempted to explain their reason for this eye-catching attire, writing that these "hereticks"

> pretended to imitate Adam's nakedness before the fall, believing themselves as innocent, and therefore [would] meet together naked upon all occasions, asserting that if Adam had not sinned, there would have been no marriages.

Not surprisingly, a humorous companion term of the same period for women who worshipped in a similar manner was *Evite*. Journalist Joseph Addison suggested, in an article in a 1713 edition of *The Guardian*, that "The Evites daily increase [so] that fig-leaves are shortly coming into fashion." An Adamite once wrote, "The sun plays so warmly upon us that some people, who were of no religion before, talk of turning Adamites in their own defense." Charles Buck's 1835 *Theological Dictionary* contained this explanation for the entry *Preadamite:* "A denomination given to the inhabitants of the earth, conceived by some people to have lived before Adam."

A variation of the story of Adam and Eve was published in the *Geneva Bible*, an edition translated into English in 1560. It was also known as the "Breeches Bible," because the Book of Genesis contained a passage observing that Adam and Eve "sewed figge tree leaves together and made themselves breeches." For centuries, Adam's arguably unnecessary navel, which the Church argued vehemently *had* existed, was one of many topics of intellectual debate on unanswerable questions, as we learn from *Hudibras:*

> What Adam dreamt of when his bride
> Came from her closet in his side;
> If either of them had a navel,
> Who first made music malleable;
> Whether the serpent at the fall,
> Had cloven feet or none at all;
> In proper terms, such as men smatter,
> When they throw out and miss the matter,
> And prove their doctrine orthodox
> By apostolic blows and knocks;
> As if religion were intended
> For nothing else but to be mended.

Saint Adam's Day was celebrated whimsically on December 20 as an English holiday honoring the "first man."

———————

BARN-BISHOP * Old English expression (wherein *barn* meant boy) for a traditional holiday dignitary—associated with the legend of Saint Nicholas of Bari—who was called the "Boy-Bishop" because of his very early exhibitions of benevolence, said to have begun "in infancy." From time immemorial, "boy-bishops," as barn-bishops were later called, were chosen from the choirs of various churches on Saint Nicholas's Day as a reenactment of the story of Jesus teaching the doctors in the temple. The position was held for three continuous weeks, during which the boy was given the right to act as bishop in all matters except saying mass. If a barn-bishop died in office, he was even afforded the full burial ceremony normally reserved for true bishops. George Puttenham, in his 1589 *Art of English Poesy*, said of them,

> Me thinks this fellow speaks like Bishop Nicholas, for on
> St. Nicholas' night, commonly the scholars of the country
> make them a bishop who, like a foolish boy, goeth about
> blessing and preaching with such childish terms as to
> make people laugh at foolish counterfeit speeches.

Christmas-lords, dignitaries similar to barn-bishops, were more commonly known as *Kings of Misrule*. Each year, during medieval and Tudor times, a boy presided over a three-month holiday season that ran from All Hallows Day until Christmas. According to Brewer's 1870 *Dictionary of Phrase and Fable*, these mock officials

> had 20–100 officers under them, furnished with hobby-
> horses, dragons and musicians, and contributed much in
> terms of a festive atmosphere. They disrupted church
> services with such babble that no one could hear his own
> voice.

In the 1550s, Queen Elizabeth abolished the odd customs of the barn-bishops and Christmas-lords, which can be traced to the ninth-century Greek Church.

———

DOG-FLOGGER * A *beadle*, or minor church official, from at least the sixteenth century until 1861, whose duty it was to supervise and discipline the unruly canines that traditionally accompanied their owners to English church services. In order to keep the peace and eject the troublemakers, these ushers sometimes employed a pair of "dog-tongs." John Atkinson, in his 1891 *Forty Years in a Moorland Parish*, elaborated on the dog-whipper, as this official was also called:

> A parish official whose duties consisted in expelling any
> dog . . . which might intrude into the church during the
> performance of any service. The office usually joined with

that of the sexton and pew-opener. The short, stout dog-whip was a regular part of the dog-whipper's equipment. . . . The office has existed down to the year 1861 and has become almost hereditary in one family.

In his 1736 *York Antiquities*, Francis Drake recalled that during the era of the dog-flogger, when Saint Luke's Day was observed in York as "Dog-whipping Day," he witnessed "a strange custom that school-boys use here of whipping all the dogs that are seen in the streets that day." This activity commemorated the occasion when a dog who had been lying under the altar swallowed a mishandled consecrated wafer, which had fallen nearby. Drake added this *post-mortem:* "The profanation of this high mystery occasioned the death of the dog, and a persecution began and has continued to this day, to be carried on against his whole tribe in our city." Church records indicate that in 1725, a Mr. John Rudge posthumously bequeathed twenty shillings per year to his parish so that they could hire a dog-flogger, who was also charged with keeping parishioners awake during services.

13. *The Body*

Bowelhives, Glisters, and Bosom-Serpents

TOOTH-FEE * An ancient Nordic custom of presenting a gift to an infant upon the appearance of its first tooth, an alternate Viking version of the "tooth-fairy" tradition. Amber, the crystallized sap of ancient trees, was also used into the twentieth century by Baltic tribes as a charm to encourage the cutting of an infant's teeth, along with teething necklaces made of peony roots. In the 1600s, a popular necklace "for easing children in breeding and cutting teeth without pain," was employed, according to its maker, the ironically named Englishman John Choke, "when they are over two months old and to wear them until they have bred all their teeth and none are troubled with the Evil or Falling Sickness." Shortly following the Choke necklace came "Chamberlain's Anodyne [pain-killer] necklace," which promised that a "secret harmony and sympathy was created between the necklace and the human body."

Elaborate superstitions developed regarding children's teeth in England, including these collected by E. M. Wright:

> When a child's tooth comes out, it must be dropped into the fire, and rhyme repeated, or the child will have to seek the tooth after death. . . . Another idea is that unless the tooth is burned, the one which grows in its place will prove a dog's tooth. If a baby's first tooth appears in the upper jaw . . . it may mean that the child will die in infancy.

Carelessness in this regard, said the 1878 *Folk-Lore Record of Sussex*, might have caused some mysterious dental problems:

Should they be found and gnawed by any animal, the child's new teeth would be . . . like the animal's that had bitten the old one. Master Simmons . . . had a very large pig's tooth in his upper jaw . . . that he feared was caused by his mother's having thrown one of his cast teeth away by accident in the hog-trough.

To avoid this problem, Frederick Ellsworthy wrote in *The Evil Eye* in 1895 that "women used to hide them in their back hair. This was done to prevent enemies or dogs getting hold of them." In his *Natural History*, Pliny wrote of protective measures used to ensure proper tooth development:

A wolf's tooth, attached to the body . . . acts as a preservative against the maladies attendant upon dentition. . . . The first teeth shed by a horse, attached as an amulet to infants, facilitates dentition, and are better still when not allowed to touch the ground.

Healing superstitions and charms were by no means confined to the uneducated and underprivileged. In 1713, for example, fifteen hundred years after Pliny, aristocratic Lady Wentworth wrote to her son that she had sent to Ireland for the same charm, a wolf's tooth, for her granddaughter, Lady Anne: "None ever breeds their teeth ill that has a wolf's tooth. I had one for all you."

ELF-LOCKS * Noun from Shakespeare's time meaning "an entanglement of the hair so thorough as to not be undone." This disarrangement, similarly employed on horses' manes and tails, was also referred to as *elf-knots*, and was said to be the spiteful amusement of Queen Mab and her night fairy subjects. On a number of occasions, Shakespeare referred to this folklore, as in *King Lear*, when Edgar says,

Brought near to beast, my face I'll grime with filth,
Blanket my loins, elf all my hair in knots.

A further account of Mab is given in *Romeo and Juliet* by Mercutio:

This is that very Mab that plaits the manes of horses in
    the night;
And bakes the elf-locks in foul sluttish hairs,
Which once untangled much misfortune bodes.

Elves were thought to be the cause of a variety of nuisances, ranging from *elf-disease* to *elf-shot*, a Scotch-Irish concept in which elves shot flint-headed arrows at cattle. In 1721, Ramsay addressed the phenomenon of being

Bewitch'd, shot by fairies. Country people tell odd tales
of this distemper among cows. When elf-shot, the cow
falls down suddenly dead; no part of the skin is pierced
but often a little triangular flat stone is found near the
beast, as they report, which is called the elf's arrow.

Nineteenth-century folklorist William Henderson reported in 1879 that elves were still engaged in their mischief:

A few years ago a ploughman in Ettrick Forest . . . heard
a whizzing sound . . . and looking up, perceived a stone
aimed at one of his horses. . . . It fell by the animal's side.
. . . He picked up the stone, but found the angles so sharp
that they cut his hand.

Walter Gregor's 1881 *Folklore of Scotland* mentioned that fairy darts

. . . were coveted as sure bringers of success, provided
they were not allowed to fall to the ground. When an
animal died suddenly, the canny woman of the district

was sent for to search for the "faery dart" and in due course she found one.

E. M. Wright wrote that in order to remedy "elf-shotten cattle" they somehow must be made to drink water into which these projectiles had been dipped, adding about elves:

> People suddenly seized with rheumatism, lumbago, paralysis or fits were supposed to have been shot at by malicious fairies, and when a prehistoric arrowhead of flint was picked up, it was alleged to be the fairy weapon, the awf-shot or fairy dart.

A tenth-century manuscript told how to give an elf-shot horse a new lease on life:

> . . . take a knife of which the haft [handle] is horn of a fallow ox, and on which are three brass nails, then write upon the horse's forehead Christ's mark, and on each of the limbs which thou may feel at; then take the left ear, prick a hole in it in silence . . . then take a yard [-stick], strike the horse on the back; then it will be whole.

At the turn of the last century, J. G. Campbell's *Superstitions of the Highlands* included precautions for keeping unwanted pests away, such as "The door posts were sprinkled with maistir, urine kept for washing purposes—a liquid extremely offensive to the fairies."

TARANTISMUS ✳ Latinesque name for a dancing mania of sixteenth- and seventeenth-century Italy, recorded in Hunter's nineteenth-century dictionary as

> . . . originating in an exaggerated dread of . . . the bite of the tarantula. The disease consisted in the sufferer ["tar-

antari"] being attacked with extreme somnolency [drowsiness] which could only be overcome by music and dancing.

Blount gave a contemporary account of the offending insect, calling it "A most venomous spider, so called of Tarentum, a neopolitan city where most abound, whose sting is deadly, yet curable by divers sounds of musick." This strange malady and cure were not without precedence, however. Beginning in the fourteenth century, Italian sufferers of a mysterious "falling sickness" (probably Sydenham's chorea), and related ailments such as epilepsy, became convinced that a cure could be had by engaging in a vigorous "writhing and hopping movement" they called *St. Vitus's Dance*. The involuntary, puppetlike motions of victims became widely imitated as a type of home remedy or prevention for myriad illnesses. They were even encouraged by well-meaning clergy who collected their donations, as we learn from Naogeorgus:

> The next is Vitus sodde [boiled] in oyle, before whose
> ymage faire
> Both men and women bringing hennes for offring do
> repaire;
> The cause whereof I do not know, I thinke for some
> disease
> Which he is thought to drive away from such as him do
> please.

The dancing myth was perpetuated by the fact that after dancers collapsed from exhaustion, symptoms of chorea were sometimes temporarily dissipated. Vitus's popularity skyrocketed during the fourteenth to sixteenth centuries among the sick and among dancers and actors, for whom he served as patron. Blount later attempted an explanation: "His dance is a kinde of madness . . . from a malignant humour gendered in the body, of near kin with the poison of the tarantula." In the eighteenth century, tarantismus gave rise to the English verb *tarantulate*, meaning, according to Skeat, "to excite or govern emotions by music."

BAKERLEGGED * Eighteenth-century term for an anatomical deformation ascribed to bakers by Halliwell, who mentioned a second baking-induced problem, being *baker-knee'd*, said of "one whose knees knocked together in walking, as if kneading dough." Bakers, once jocularly known as "burn-crusts," were said to be especially vulnerable to knee problems, especially one in which their knees typically bent slightly backward due to prolonged standing while making bread. "Bakerlegged" was used as early as 1607, as is evident from a rhetorical question posed in Thomas Dekker's play, *Westward Hoe:* "Will women's tongues, like bakers' legs, never go straight?" Records also indicate that bakers' feet were often "twisted, badly-shaped or distorted." This attribute, considered a bad omen even to witness, appeared in Lewis Machin's 1608 play, *The Dumbe Knight:*

> Sure I said my prayers, ris'd on my right side,
> Wash'd my hands and eyes, put on my girdle last;
> Sure I met no splay-footed baker,
> No hare did cross me, nor no bearded witch,
> Nor other ominous sign.

A male baker's or bakester's female counterpart was once called a *backstress*, which unintentionally but appropriately sounded like "back stress."

SPLEENFULL * Adjective from the sixteenth and seventeenth centuries meaning passionate. Beginning about the fourteenth century, many believed that laughter and temperament originated with the spleen, as we hear from Armando in Shakespeare's *Love's Labour's Lost:*

> By virtue, thou enforcest laughter; thy silly thought, my spleen; the heaving of my lungs provokes me to ridiculous smiling.

Similarly, John Donne wrote in 1631, "Laughter is the [hiccup] of a foolish spleen." This organ was also blamed for "splenitive" mood swings, depression, melancholy, anger, and morose feelings, and gave rise to the popular expression "venting one's spleen." Shakespeare developed the impetuous character, Hotspur in *Henry IV,* who was "governed by a spleen," and wrote in *Henry VIII,* "Your heart is cramm'd with arrogancy, spleen and pride." In *Hudibras,* yet other emotions are linked with the spleen, as well as its "sister organ," the stomach:

> This stirr'd his spleen
> More than the danger he was in,
> Honour, despight [contempt], revenge and shame,
> At once into his stomach came.

Mustard was considered one of the best tonics for the spleen and other organs, as we learn from Gerarde's *Herbal:*

> Mustard is an excellent sauce for those whose blood wants clarifying, and for weak stomachs. The seed, taken by itself in an electuary or drink, doth mightily stir up bodily lust, and helps the spleen and pains in the sides, and gnawing in the bowels.

Another old remedy for the spleen required the doctor to

> Take an ounce of the filings of steel, two drachms of gentian sliced, half an ounce of carduus seeds bruised, half a handful of centaury tops; infuse all these in a quart of white wine four days; drink four spoonfuls of the clear

every morning, fasting two hours after it and walking about. If it binds too much, take once or twice a week some purging thing to carry it off.

Stomachfull, a companion word to spleenfull of the same period, indicated pride or stubbornness. Queen Elizabeth was probably referring to the former trait when she told her troops: "I know I have the body of a weak and feeble woman, but I have the . . . stomach of a king." Bloodletting (see *Fleam*, page 21), often associated with the spleen, was once a fashionable means of ridding oneself of the "bad blood" that was thought to induce these unpleasant emotions.

FOTADL ✱ Literally "foot disease" in Old English, or more precisely gout. Mention of it can be found as early as Chaucer's *Canterbury Tales*, in which he alluded to the belief of his day that this swelling of the ankle and foot joints was caused by "morbid humours" in the blood, causing pain and immobility. An Old French word related to gout, *gautier*, a "conductor of

water," gave rise to the English word *gutter*. In the seventeenth century, reflecting the physical slowing of fluids that accompanies gout, the term *gout-justice* was used to mean an outcome that seemed hopelessly delayed. Dew found on the grass on May Day had its place in the seventeenth-century physician's arsenal for gout, as Aubrey wrote in his 1691 *Natural History of Wiltshire:*

> Maydewe is a very great dissolvent of many things . . . that will not be dissolved any other way, which puts me in mind of the rationality of the method used by William Gore, Esq. for his gout, which was to walk in the dew with his shoes pounced [perforated]; he found benefit in it.

Gout, which is often caused or intensified by the consumption of red wine and rich foods, was so common that by the nineteenth century, mass-produced *gout-stools,* for elevating an affected foot, were introduced to help patients "disgout" their swollen feet. E. M. Wright cataloged other methods for relieving symptoms of gout:

> Wear eel-skin garters, especially when bathing; sleep with your stockings on, and with a piece of sulphur in each; [and] go to bed with the skin of a mole bound around your left thigh; carry in . . . a little bag tied around your neck . . . the top vertebra of a goose.

When conventional remedies proved unsuccessful, a "transplant," as found in Thomas Browne's 1672 *Pseudodoxia Epidemica,* warranted consideration:

> Since you are so unsatisfied with the many rationall medicines which you . . . have tried for gout, you have leasure enough to make triall of these empericall medicines. . . . Trie the way of transplantation. . . . Give pultesses taken from the [gouty] part unto doggs, & lett a whelp lye in the bed with you.

Benjamin Franklin believed that sexual intercourse "on a regular basis" would prevent gout.

LEECH-FINGER * A doctor's so-called "medical finger" (*leech* meant physician), translated literally from Latin *digitus medicus*. Since Greek and Roman times, the "lytell seconde fynger," or ring finger, was believed to be endowed with an

increased capacity of *felth* (Anglo-Saxon for "palpatory sensation"), especially when it touched something harmful. The "sixth sense" was attributed to a special nerve thought to run directly from that finger, called the *annularis* in 1700, to the heart. This anatomical mythology formed the basis for wearing a wedding ring on the third finger of the left hand, a custom which originated at least as early as the 1100s. For centuries, betrothal rings were never removed, as Brand explained:

> Many married women are so rigid, not to say superstitious, in their notions concerning their wedding rings that neither when they wash their hands, nor at any other time, will they take it from their finger, extending, it

should seem, the expression of "till death us do part" even to this golden circlet, the token and pledge of matrimony.

A vascular variation of this belief was presented by Henry Swinburne in his 1686 *Treatise of Spousals:*

> The finger on which the [wedding] ring is to be worn . . . by the opinion of the learned in ripping up and anatomising men's bodies, there is a vein of blood, called the *vena amoris,* which passeth from that finger to the heart.

In *Secret Miracles of Nature,* Lemnius shared an eighteenth-century trick he used to energize himself and his friends when fatigued:

> I use to raise such as are fallen in a swoon by pinching this [leech-finger] joynt, and by rubbing the ring of gold with a little saffron, for by this a restoring force that is in it, passeth to the heart and refresheth the fountain of life, unto which this finger is join'd.

The same finger was used for centuries by apothecaries when mixing herbal remedies, some very poisonous in sufficient quantity. Lemnius notes that to avoid serving up a lethal dose, they "would mingle their medicaments and potions with this finger, for no venom can stick upon the outmost part of it, but it will offend a man and communicate itself to the heart." As late as the twentieth century, this finger was used by English physicians to stroke wounds and sores for curative purposes.

PILGARLICK ✻ Sixteenth-century word for a bald head, suggestive of peeled garlic. A bald man was also termed a pilgarlick at this time, especially following an illness, as hair loss was believed an outcome of pathology. A recipe from this period advised:

> Take of boar's-grease two ounces, ashes of southernwood, juice of white lily-root, oil of sweet almonds, of each one drachm; six drachms of pure musk; and according to an art, make an ointment of these; and the day before the full moon, shave the place, anointing it every day with this ointment; it will cause hair to grow.

Water "distilled from human hair" and mixed with honey was touted by seventeenth-century doctors as a hair restorative. Culpepper offered hope for the pilgarlick with an equally appealing technique: "Beat Linseeds very well, and mix them with Sallad-oil; and when you have mixed them, anoint the head therewith, and in three or four times using, it will help you." In his *Herbal* he recommended alternative treatments for baldness, such as an application of bear's grease, "froth of the sea . . . [which] trimly decks the head with hair," and another: "The brain of an hare being roasted helps . . . [the] falling off of hair, the head being anointed with it." In cutting regenerated hair, timing was everything:

> Crop your hair in the moon's wax,
> Na'er cut it in the wane,
> And then of a bald head
> You shall never complain.

Halliwell presented another product for treatment of "the mange," called "shab-water," a "tonic made of tobacco and "mercuria" used to treat shab." The modern adjective "bold-faced," used in referring to a lie or its perpetrator, was corrupted slightly from *bald-faced*, which formerly meant "white-faced from shame."

TYMPANE * An intestinal affliction, according to Blount, whereby "the belly swells up, having great store of windy humours . . . which being smitten with the hand, makes a noise like a tabor." Thomas Paynell's *Book of Health* later described the tympane as being "engendered by coldnes of the stomake and lyver, not suffering mans drynke or meate to be converted in to good humours, but tourneth them to ventuosities [flatulence]." Jamieson wrote of a similar condition, which the nineteenth-century Scots called by the instinctively understandable name "bowelhive," alluding to a buzzy intestinal disorder perhaps akin sensorially to "butterflies in the stomach." He speculated bowelhive might have been caused by "one part of the intestines being inverted." Jamieson quoted Curtis's *Medical Observer* as stating that bowelhive "is brought on by . . . exposure to cold, and living in low, cold, damp situations." Formed from the Greek word from which we took the modern name for an orchestral kettledrum, this disorder, according to Dunglison's 1844 *Medical Dictionary*, when symptomatic, "is usually fatal." And one woman, as recorded by Holinshed's *Chronicles*, "was deceived by a tympanie . . . to thinke hirselfe with child."

Before the advent of convenient antacids, homemade remedies were literally whipped up to counteract bloating after meals, such as this "Electuary for a cold or windy stomach" of the 1700s:

> Take gum-guaiacum one ounce, cubebs and cardamums, of each a quarter of an ounce; beat and sift all these, and mix it with syrup of gilliflowers into an electuary. Take night and morning the quantity of a nutmeg; drink a little warm ale after it.

The *Fairfax Household Book* gave an indispensable royal recipe, Queen Elizabeth's "Potion for Wind," containing ginger, cinnamon, mace, nutmeg, galingale, aniseeds, caraway seeds, fennel seeds, and white sugar. *The Queen's Closet Opened* of 1655 gave a very different recipe for that ailment: "A powder for the wind in the body [containing] goose horns, capons and pigeons."

BESPAWL * Popular seventeenth-century verb for an insulting gesture, meaning specifically to "bespatter with saliva," whose origins are obscure. English writers of this period, including John Milton, Ben Jonson, and Michael Drayton, used this poetically colorful variant of spit, taken from the Anglo-Saxon *spittan*, "to eject from the mouth," and the Latin *sputum*, a medical word still used for oral and respiratory fluids. In *The Discovery of Witchcraft*, Scot suggested a protective use for saliva:

> To unbewitch the bewitched, you must spit in the pot where you have made water. Otherwise spit into the shoe of your right foot before you put it on; that . . . is good and wholesome to do before you go into any dangerous place.

When a boy was said to be a "spitting image" of his father, it probably never meant that he expectorated in a similar manner. Harold Wentworth suggested that spit was an American corruption of spirit, and that the phrase may have originated as "spirit and image." Hazlitt explained that an old nurses' custom of *lustrating*, or cleaning children with spittle,

> . . . was one of the ceremonies used on the Dies Nominalis, the day the child was named; so that there can be no doubt of the Papists deriving this custom from the heathen nurses and grand-mothers; but then they carried it to a more filthy extravagance by daubing it on the nostrils of adults as well as of children.

Lemnius explained a curious benefit enjoyed by those who availed themselves of the spit of a faster:

Divers experiments shew what power and quality there is in man's fasting spittle, when he hath neither eat nor drunk before the use of it; for it cures all tetters, itch, scabs and creeping sores; and if venomous little beasts have fastened on any part of the body, as hornets, beetles, toads, spiders and such like, that by their venom cause tumours and great pains and inflammations, do but rub the places with fasting spittle, and all those effects will be gone and dispersed.

Money from a witch was once mingled with saliva as a precautionary measure. Henderson warned:

Should you receive money from a witch, put it at once into your mouth, for fear the donor should spirit it away and supply its place with a round stone. . . . Old people constantly put into their mouths the money which is paid them.

Robinson told of a method employed in Leeds to bring good luck: "When a coin has been given, or comes somewhat unexpectedly, it is spit upon for luck before it goes into the pocket." A *spitting-stock* in the late 1700s was the equivalent of a laughingstock, an object of ridicule.

BOSOM-SERPENT * A person treated with kindness and affection who in return inflicted an emotionally venomous wound. A similar seventeenth-century expression was *bosom-cheat*, which had a less religiously dramatic connotation. Perhaps the first recorded reference to the bosom-serpent in literature is found in *A Midsummer-Night's Dream*, when Hermia wakes from a nightmare screaming to her lover,

Help me, Lysander, help me! Do thy best
To pluck this crawling serpent from my breast. . . .

Methought a serpent eat my heart away,
And you sat smiling at his cruel prey.

These victims of their own benevolence sometimes resorted to erecting what was termed in the eighteenth century a *bosom-barrier*, a form of psychological protection against the onslaughts of human selfishness. Others developed a *bosom-vice*, a favorite forbidden activity such as gambling or drinking. Human "venom" was not only injurious to kindly people but, in an amazing turn of the tables, was believed to kill snakes until the eighteenth century, as we learn from Pliny:

> All men possess in their bodies a poison which acts upon serpents, and the human saliva, it is said, makes them take to flight [and] destroys them the moment it enters their throat, and more particularly so, if it . . . be the saliva of a man who is fasting.

E. M. Wright provided a pair of local remedies for physical snakebites: "a poultice compounded of boiled onions and rotten eggs . . . [and] repeat verses one and two of Psalm 68 . . . as a protection from adders and as a cure for their bites." Perhaps the most twisted and bizarre manifestation of the bosom-serpent was an eighteenth-century ploy called "wolf in the breast." It was used by vagrant English women with considerable courage and acting talent to elicit kindness from the gullible by faking a breast disorder. This macabre ruse consisted of the beggar pretending to be in severe pain because of a small wolf, which the woman attempted to convince passersby was gnawing her "from inside."

EXCREMENT * Anything that grew from or on the human body, including fingernails, beard, or hair, during the 1500s and 1600s. It was derived from the Latin *excrescere*, "that which comes forth," and in this context, William Hull in 1615 described silver and gold as "white and yellow excrements of the earth." In Shakespeare's *Love's Labour's Lost*, Armando boasts of his close relationship with the king, saying that his majesty would "with his royal finger thus dallie with my excrement, with my mustachio." A favorite pleasure of seventeenth-century Dutch scholar Isaac Vossius was having his hair combed:

> Many people take an odd delight in the rubbing of their limbs and the combing of their hair, but these exercises would delight much more if the servants of the baths . . . were so skilful in this art that they would express any measure with their fingers. I have fallen into the hands of men of this sort, who could initiate . . . songs in combing the hair . . . from whence there arose in me no small delight.

The type of excrement known as the beard has been both hailed and shunned in the history of fashion. Henry Bohn wrote in 1860 that fashion-conscious men "in the reigns of James I and Charles I, spent as much time in dressing their beards as modern beaux do in dressing their hair; and many kept a person to read to them while the operation was performing." On the other end of the spectrum, Russia's eighteenth-century czar, Peter the Great, in an attempt to eliminate beards, imposed a "beard tax" upon subjects and visitors entering the capital. His reasoning, one hopes, was better than that of Thomas Randolph, who, in his 1638 *Amyntas*, advised: "Above all things, wear no beard; long beards are signs the brains are full, because the excrements come out so plentifully." Although much arm hair was a sign of certain wealth, the principle that an abundance of scalp hair signified a lack of brains led to the expression "Bush natural, more hair than wit."

YELDER-EE'D * "Evil-eyed," from Scottish, as explained by Jamieson: "This provincial term seems to have great antiquity, being evidently allied to Anglo-Saxon 'gealdercraeftas,' a term used to denote those who were supposed to exercise the magical arts." Until the 1700s, people with unusual ocular characteristics were considered to be possessed by demons and sometimes "treated" by being tied to a large carved crucifix in a church to assure that they absorbed the service, or by having a cross shaved onto their heads. Apparently nobody was exempt from eye-altering devils, as Hazlitt reported that even nineteenth-century Pope Pius IX "was said to have the 'evil eye,' and when he blessed people, some would avert their faces and spit to avoid the spell." The Book of Proverbs cautioned against buying bread from certain bakers: "Eat not the bread of him that hath an evil eye."

Hunchbacks have long been regarded as capable of protecting people from effects of the evil eye. Since medieval times, they were retained for this purpose by kings and nobility, sometimes being depicted in castings and carvings that were carried as charms. Culpeper offered this remedy to his readers with less severe eye problems:

> Take of Fennel, Eyebright, Roses, Celandine, Vervain and
> Rue, of each a handful, [and] the liver of a goat chopt
> small; infuse them well in Eyebright-water, then distil
> them well in an alembic, and you shall have a water that
> will clear the sight beyond comparison.

Dr. Andry described a weird condition no longer treated by eye-doctors called "The Haggard," or "Fierce Eye":

> The deformity is commonly the effect of a bad education,
> from allowing children to look angry at those who contradict them, or refuse to give them everything they ask.

A prudent governess will check the haughty temper of a child which a foolish mother gives way to. When a child sees himself encouraged in their humours, he becomes more proud, haughty and ill-natured.

An eighteenth-century method "to clear the eyes" called for the sufferer to "Take the white of hens-dung, dry it very well, and beat it to powder; sift, and blow it into the eyes when the party goes to bed."

14. Drink Hail!

Balderdash, Sillyebubbe, and Crapulence

CYMMHORTH * Medieval Welsh term indicating an ale-drinking benefit held for various purposes, such as a *bride-ale*, a wedding reception, the proceeds from which were given to the newlywed couple. In the fifteenth to seventeenth centuries, *bid-ales* were held wherein "an honest man decayed in his estate [is] set up again by the liberal benevolence and contribution of friends at a feast, to which those friends are bid or invited." A *clerk-ale*, or *give-ale*, was an affair held during the Easter holidays, which was intended to ease the clerk's job of collecting contributions for church repairs or honoring a patron saint, until this festival was reported in 1678 to have been used by the clerk "for his private benefit and the solace of his neighborhood." The *audit-ale* was a strong brew made, according to Dr. Brewer,

> . . . at some of the Oxford and Cambridge colleges, and originally broached on audit day when college accounts had to be paid up by the students. Whether this was intended as a consolation to the students or a mild form of celebration by the college authorities is uncertain.

Jamieson reported that in Scotland another cymmhorth, the *fute-ale* (pronounced "fit-ale"), was "A sort of entertainment given to those present when a woman, who has borne a child, for the first time gets out of bed." Blount wrote of yet another type, called the *Mountain of Pity:*

> A stock of money raised by charity of good people who, observing the poor ruined by usury . . . voluntarily con-

tributed good store of treasure to be preserved and lent
to them, whereby they might have money at a low rate
to relieve their wants.

Cymmhorths of the fifteenth century influenced the development of the modern trade union, in which workers in their
particular fields gathered to work on common projects and discuss grievances. Because of the camaraderie they engendered in
their participants, especially those spiced with the influence of
drink and traveling entertainers, the focus of cymmhorths grad-
ually shifted to sociopolitical realms, sometimes assuming ide-
ological positions. In response to a perceived threat by these

dissident organizations, Welsh rulers decreed "that no westrye,
rhymer, minstrel, nor vagabond be in any [way] sustained in
the land of Wales to make cymmorthas or gatherings upon the
common people." The cymmhorth was finally outlawed during
the sixteenth-century English Reformation.

METHEGLIN ✳ A style of *mead,* or spiced, "medicated,"
honey wine, originally produced in Wales. One old recipe re-
veals that herbs used in its creation included thyme, sage, oreg-
ano, hyssop, rosemary, and others. In an 1179 manuscript,

Giraldus Cambrensis put metheglin in a category with the finest liquors available, saying that at feasts

> You might see in the midst of such abundance, wine and strong drink, metheglin and claret, must, mead and mulberry juice, and all that can intoxicate; beverages so choice that beer, such as is made at its best in England and above all in Kent, found no place among them.

Dyche explained how to make this "very pleasant and wholesome liquor":

> Put as much live honey, naturally running from the comb into spring water, as that when it is thoroughly dissolved an egg will stand suspended in it; then boil it so long as that it will swim a small matter above the surface. When cool, put to every 15 gallons, of ginger, cloves, and mace, each one ounce, and of cinnamon, half an ounce, all grossly broken; and to promote the working, add a small quantity of yeast. After it has done working, let it stand one month to settle, and then draw it off in bottles.

The prefix *methe* was once a Welsh term for both mead and healing, as well as a Greek word for intoxication. Combined with the suffix *llyn*, liquor, metheglin literally meant "healing and intoxicating honey-liquor," although Shakespeare grouped metheglin with some questionable bedfellows in *The Merry*

Wives of Windsor: "He is given to fornications and to taverns, and sack, and wine, and metheglins, and to drinkings, and swearings, pribbles and prabbles."

STIRRUP-CUP * Cup of wine or other liquor handed to a seventeenth-century man on horseback before his departure from an inn, an activity which has since become known as "one for the road." In Scotland, this activity was called a *stirrup-*

dram or, in Gaelic, "deoch an doruis," literally "drink of the door." Fortunately, at that time a horse was often capable of seeing his rider safely home without guidance, if necessary. An accompanying piece of scintillating poetry, such as this excerpt from Sir Walter Scott's *Bride of Lammermoor,* was similarly deemed a *stirrup-verse:*

> Look not thou on beauty's charming,
> Sit thou still when kings are arming,
> Taste not when the wine cup glistens,
> Speak not when the people listens,

Vacant heart and hand, and eye,
Easy live and quiet die.

By the nineteenth century, the meaning of stirrup-cup was expanded to include the welcoming of a guest with a drink before his dismount, and was applied to the cup as well.

SILLYEBUBBE * One of many spellings for a popular English beverage of the 1500s to the 1800s, whose suffix, *bub*, denoted a frothy beverage said "to coole a cholerick stomacke." Originally, it was made by milking a cow directly into spiced cider or wine, thereby curdling the milk, and whipping it with a *froathstick*. It is recorded that bridegrooms frequently imbibed sillyebubbe, assuredly for its calming effects. *The Compleat Cook* of 1671 listed the following recipe for *Cyder-Syllabub*:

> Fill your pot with cyder and good store of sugar and a little nutmeg; stir it well together and put in as much thick cream as you put cyder, by two or three spoonfulls at a time. Then stir all exceedingly softly once about and let stand two hours at least ere it is eaten, for the standing makes it curd.

Another recipe from this book called for the cook to

> Take a quart and a half pint of cream, a pint of rhenish [German wine], half a pint of sack, three lemons and near a pound of double refined sugar; beat and sift the sugar, and put it to your cream; grate off the yellow rind of your three lemons into your wine, and put that to your cream, then beat all together with a whisk just half an hour; then take it all together with a spoon and fill your glasses with it. It will keep good nine days, and is best three or four days old; these are call'd the "everlasting syllabubs."

A dessert drink of ale, wine, or even lime juice, and hot or cold curdled milk with sugar and spices, called a *posset*, was recommended by doctors to ward off illnesses such as colds, and was frequently drunk by newlyweds as a nightcap. A posset recipe from *The Compleat Housewife* was made as follows:

> Take a quart of cream and mix it with a pint of ale, then beat the yolks of ten eggs and the whites of four; when they are well-beaten, put them to the cream and ale; sweeten it to your taste and slice some nutmeg in it; set it over the fire and keep it stirring all the while; when it is thick and before it boils, take it off and pour it into the bason you serve it to the table.

Warm milk, "straight from the cow," was once a fashionable drink served in seventeenth- and eighteenth-century health resorts, such as Bagnigge Wells, near London. Among James Howell's *Familiar Letters* of 1645 is one entreating a friend to join him:

> If you are in health, 'tis well, wee are here all so, and wee should be better had wee your company; therefore I pray leave the smutty ayr of London and com hither to breath sweeter, where you may pluck a rose and drink cillibub.

By the 1700s, sillyebubbe's frothiness came to figuratively represent a discourse or writing that lacked substance.

BIBULOUS * In the seventeenth century, a word that meant "absorbent, like a sponge," later used figuratively to mean "addicted to alcohol," having the same source as *imbibe*. At that time, a *bib* was a cloth associated with wine *bibulation* and was worn to keep "tears of the tankard" from dripping on the tippler's waistcoat. *Bybbe*, from the same Latin root *bibo*, to drink, referred to the clever subterfuge of drinking small, frequent sips of liquor at brief intervals, amounting to a large aggregate, without the appearance of excess, while *bibacity* de-

noted an outrageous drinking capacity. Seventeenth-century poet Dean Aldrich seems to have had all the rationales he needed for drinking beer:

> If all be true that I do think,
> There are five reasons we should drink:
> Good beer, a friend, or being dry,
> Or lest we should be, by and by,
> Or any other reason why.

Brand's *Popular Antiquities* mentioned a punishment for the sin of "excess quaffing":

> It appears . . . that in the time of the Commonwealth, the magistrates of Newcastle-upon-Tyne punished . . . drunkards by making them carry a tub with holes in the sides for the arms to pass through, called [a] Drunkard's Cloak, through the streets of that town.

Saint Bibiana was the fourth-century Spanish patron saint of hangover sufferers. A church was erected on the site of her death, around which grew an unnamed herb that reportedly reduced the effects of liquor overindulgence. Her name was a Spanish version of Viviana, with "V" pronounced as an English "B." As such, her name was thought to mean "heavy drinker," instead of the more correct Latin translation, "vivacious," which contributed to her unusual patronage.

ALE-CONNOR * An appointed English official, in functional existence from about the eleventh to eighteenth centuries, whose duty was to sample ale for quality and, after doing so, dictate what could be charged for it. In a test administered

to screen for excessive sweetness or illegal additives, this inspector visited an ale-house, ordered a pint, and poured some of it on his bench. He sat in the ale for thirty minutes, then arose. If the bench stuck to his leather breeches, the tavern owner could be fined for serving *taplash*, an inferior ale. Nares reported that in some locales,

> . . . the ale-connor's jurisdiction was very extensive, authorized to search for, destroy, seize and take away all unwholesome provisions, false balances, short weights and measures, to enter the brewhouses and examine the quality of ale and the materials of which it is made.

An example of the rules under which brewers were licensed is found in this passage by Brother William Geryn, cellarer of the Abbey of Cokersand, in 1326:

> There shall no brewer let no tenant for to have ale for their silver out of their house, and such [may] have four gallons within their house, [if] they bring a vessel with them. Ye shall not sell a gallon of ale above a halfpenny when ye may buy a quarter of good oats for two pence. Ye shall give ale-founders [forerunners of ale-connors] a founding-gallon, or else a taste of each vessel . . . on pain of grievous amerciaments.

In a passage from the 1630 *Tincker of Turvey*, it appears that the ale-connor's authority was sometimes circumvented by skillfully devious brewers: "The autenticall drinke of England, the whole barmy-tribe of ale-cunners never layd their lips to the like." As the ale-connor's job was a coveted one, false inspectors seeking bribes or free beer were common.

CRAPULENCE * An eighteenth-century term that denoted intestinal and cranial distress humorously referred to as "barrel fever," arising from intemperance and debauchery. From the Latin root *crapula*, itself adapted from a Greek word *craepale*, it meant, according to Galen, "A derangement of the functions of the brain, produced by wine or other fermented liquor." *Cropsick*, although etymologically unrelated, was a synonym from the same period. Rudyard Kipling described having once been cropsick:

> I've a head like a concertina,
> I've a tongue like a button-stick,
> I've a mouth like an old potato,
> And I'm more than a little sick.

A passage from *The Homish Apothecary* analyzed people's varying sensitivity to alcohol:

> It chanceth sometime to some folk to be drunken and yet do not drink overmuch, and that happeneth two manners of ways. First that they have had so great pain or wept so much that thereby their brains are become feeble; and when they drink the drinking doth so much the sooner strike their brains. Or else they have a feeble head and brains.

In Shakespeare's *Othello*, Cassio identifies himself as one of those not easily able to consume alcohol when he says,

> I have very poor and unhappy brains for drinking:
> I could well wish courtesy would invent some other cus-
>   tom of entertainment.

Fortunately for sufferers of crapulence, Culpeper's *Herbal* provided a long-term solution: "Eels, being put into wine or beer, and suffered to die in it, he that drinks it will never endure that sort of liquor again."

It was considered a blessing for some crapulence-prone ale swillers when Michaelmas fell on the last Monday of September, because on the morning of Saint Michael, sleeping late was condoned. A fair, held near Guildford, England, on *Tap-up Sunday*, the last Sunday of the month, allowed unlicensed brewers to tap their kegs and sell ale. The following old rhyme reflected this grace period, with its reference to hours of sleep:

> Nature requires five,
> Custom gives seven;
> Laziness takes nine,
> And Michaelmas eleven.

BALDERDASH * In its original meaning, dating from the sixteenth century, an odd or inappropriate combination of two or more liquors, such as ale and wine or, as found in Ben Jonson's play *New Inn*, "Beer [and] butter-milk, mingled together. . . . It is against my free-hold . . . to drink such balderdash." Another undoubtedly wretched intestinal cleansing concoction was offered with comic optimism by Thomas Heywood about 1640:

> Where sope hath fayl'd without,
> Balderdash wines within will worke no doubt.

Skeat reported that at one time balderdash was generally employed "to signify weak talk, poor poetry, &c. But it was formerly used also of adulterated or thin potations, or of frothy water." The word balderdash might have stemmed from the Anglo-Saxon *bald*, meaning bold, or from a particular style of sillyebubbe, called *balductum*, in which ale or wine was added to milk. By the seventeenth century, a verb form of this word was created which meant "to adulterate any liquor," perhaps influencing Jamieson's allusion to liquids in his definition of the noun: "Foolish, noisy talk, poured out with great fluency." The word eventually broadened to denote a ridiculous and often pretentious type of nonsense or obscene language, and is still used in this context.

LANT * Stale human urine, employed for a variety of domestic and industrial purposes from the seventeenth to nineteenth centuries, such as a cleaning agent known as "chamber lye." Lant was derived from the thousand-year-old Saxon word, *bland*, of the same meaning. James Burn, in his 1859 *Autobiog-*

raphy of a Beggar Boy, threw light on the acquisition of lant in intimating one of his least favorite childhood tasks: "Twice a-week I had to collect stale lant from a number of places where it was preserved for me." Lant was used in old recipes as an additive that moistened pastry and helped the glaze to stick, as referred to in Wilson's *Inconstant Lady:*

> A goodly peece of puff [pastry],
> A little lantified, to hold the gilding.

Another consumable application for lant was as an additive to ale, apparently for the flavor it imparted. Styles of lanted brew, referred to as *single-* or *double-lanted ale* depending on the concentration of urine, were mentioned in the 1630 *Tincker of Turvey:* "I have drunke double-lanted ale and single-lanted, but never gulped downe such Hypocrenian liquor in all my life."

Henry Glapthorne's 1640 comedy, *Wit in a Constable*, alluded to an old belief about lant's effects on the skin: "Your nose, by its complexion, does betray your frequent drinking country ale with lant in't." The work *Sylva, Or The Wood*, described a bizarre medical custom of drinking lant "straight up": "A few years ago, women in labour used to drink the urine of their husbands, who were all the while stationed, as I have seen the cows in St. James Park, and straining themselves to give as much as they can." Holland's 1656 *Wit & Fancy in a Maze* referred to yet another mysterious use of lant: "They found their eares ungented with warm water, well lanted with a viscuous ingredient." Herrick offered a lanted recipe for making a "witch-cake," used to break a witch's spell, or as it was known, "bring in the witch": "To house the hag, you must do this: Commix with meals a little pisse of him bewicht; then forthwith make a little wafer or cake and this rawly bak't will bring the old hag in. No surer thing." Three centuries ago, lant was commonly used as a barber's hair rinse, called *lotium*, and today, listed as urea, lant is an ingredient in dozens of American shampoos and skin care products. Human urine is also contained in two very expensive prescription drugs, the popular fertility enhancer, Pergonal, and a heart attack medicine, Urokinase.

OAST-HOUSE * Building with a distinctive conical roof, named from the Latin *aestas*, summer, harvest time for the pungent preservative herb called hops. Beginning in the seventeenth century, barley malt, and later hops, were kiln-dried on large horsehair blankets in oast-houses. By royal English decree, ale was long brewed without hops, scornfully referred to as the "wicked weed," until the fifteenth century. Seventeenth-century herbalists, such as Culpeper, implied that the use of hops put beer in a class with medicines: "In cleansing of blood, hops help to cure the French disease or pox, and all manners of scabs . . . tetters, ringworm and spreading sores. . . . Half a dram of the seed taken in drinks kills worms in the body." Before the 1600s, many beer-flavoring substitutes were used, such as balsam, dandelion, pine needles, mint, tansey, wormwood, coriander, and even hay. Since that time, the hop has become a venerated component of English ale and most beers brewed worldwide. An eighteenth-century song about hops tells why:

> Haste, then and strip, as it bends from the pole
> The fruit that gives vigor and strength to the soul
> Our hearts and our spirits to cheer
> It warms and enlivens the true English beer.

An old proverb makes reference to the "coming of the hop" from Holland in the year of Shakespeare's birth, 1564, about the time Henry VIII challenged the authority of the pope:

> Heresy and hops in beer
> Came into England in one year.

Hops became so popular that in the mid-nineteenth century, English laws decreed that any malicious damaging of hop vines constituted a felony. About this time, members of London's lower classes traveled to Kent during the summer to pick hops as a "working vacation."

W ASSAIL * Beverage made of sweetened ale or wine, flavored with spices and roasted apples, drunk to the health of loved ones from a two-handled *loving cup* made for simultaneous sharing. On Wassail evening, once known as *Twelfth Night*, medieval participants celebrated the conclusion of the Yule season. A fluffy spiced drink made of whipped apple pulp and ale, called *lamb's wool*, was once carried in a bowl house-to-house in Somersetshire to toast one's neighbors with, as we learn from Herrick:

> Next crowne the bowl full
> With gentle lambs-wooll;
> Adde sugar, nutmeg and ginger,
> With store of ale too;
> And thus ye must doe
> To make the wassaile a swinger.

Apple trees were serenaded with "wassailing songs," a throwback to Roman times when sacrifices were made to the goddess of apple fertility, Pomona. In a verse, Herrick suggested this was the original purpose of wassailing:

> Wassail the trees, that they may bear
> You many a plum and many a pear;
> For more or less fruits they will bring
> As you do give them wassailing.

A passage from the 1892 *Peasant Speeches of Devon* reported: "On Wassail Eve it was customary for farmers to pour large quantities of cyder on the roots of the primest apple-trees in the orchard."

The Old Norse thirteenth-century drinking salutation *waes hail*, which meant "be thou healthy," is closely related to wassail, as well as the modern English words *whole* and *holy*. (The usual reply to this toast was *"Drink hail!"*) By the sixteenth century, it had become a verb meaning to embrace; wassail eventually became the modern "vessel." Blount's *Glossographia* gave an additional clue to the word itself: "Another etymology of this word wassale [is that] common people do often, on those nights, wash their throats with ale." The clinking together of cups, and later glasses, known as *toasting*, was originally an attempt to mimic the sound of church bells, which were rung to ward off the devil. A king's glass used for a toast was often broken to prevent its use by commoners, a custom which still lives when a glass is smashed in a fireplace after toasting. The Middle English word *toast* came from the ancient custom of floating toasted and spiced bread in punch to enhance the flavor.

DEW-DRINK ✳ An early morning allowance of beer granted to nineteenth- and twentieth-century English farm laborers before beginning their harvesting efforts. This dawn libation, sometimes referred to as a *dew-cup*, reflecting the accumulation of moisture likely on the ground at the time of consumption, was sometimes accompanied by a *dew-bit*, or breakfast snack, such as *fitchet-pie*, composed of "apples, onions and the fat of bacon, in equal quantities." Beer was also the norm at the conclusion of at least the first day's work, as this excerpt from an 1826 letter detailed:

> It is a general practice on the first day of harvest for the men to leave the field about four o'clock and retire to the

alehouse, and have what is termed here a "whet," that is a sort of drinking bout to cheer their hearts for labour. They previously solicit any who happen to come within their sight with, "I hope, sir, you will please to bestow a largess upon us?" If the boon is conceded, the giver is asked if he would like to have his largess hallooed; if this is assented to, the men all "holler largess" at the tops of their voices.

At this time, *foot-ale* was a round of beer required for the whole company from a workman who entered a new job site or office, known also as "shoeing the colt." The word was fashioned from *foot*, once a fee paid as a person first "set foot" in a new place, the tradition being also called "paying the footing." These customary imbibements undoubtedly resulted in *barleyhoods*, spells of liquor-induced bad temper, the result of which was demonstrated in a verse from Andrew Scott's 1805 *Scottish Poems:*

> Whan e're they take their barley-hoods,
> And heat of fancy fires their bludes;
> Their vera kings and queens they take,
> And kill them just for killing's sake.

15. *The Final Curtain*

Manquellers, Arfnames, and Resurrectionists

SINNE-EATER * A poor person hired to absorb the sins of recently deceased souls and thereby spare them the discomforts of purgatory. Into the nineteenth century, this was accomplished by *sinne-eating*, wherein the sinne-eater would ceremonially consume food prepared by the family of the deceased, such as bread and ale, in the vicinity of the corpse. Without such a ceremony, an accumulation of transgressions would otherwise have kept the dead person's ghost "hovering round his relations on earth." Aubrey provided details about one such ritual in his 1688 *Remaines of Gentilisme:*

> In the County of Hereford was an old custome at funeralls to hire poor people who were to take upon them all the sinnes of the party deceased. The manner was that . . . a corps was brought out of the house and laid on a biere; a loafe of bread was brought out and delivered to the sinne-eater over the corps, as also a mazer-bowle full of beer, which he was to drink up, and sixpence of money, in consideration whereof he took upon him all the sinnes of the defunct, and freed him (or her) from walking after they were dead.

John Leland's 1714 *Collectanea* described the procedures of sinne-eating:

> Within the memory of our fathers in Shropshire, in those villages adjoyning to Wales, when a person dyed, there was notice given to an old Sire, who presently repaired to the place where the deceased lay, and stood before the

door of the house, when some of the family came out and furnished him with a cricket on which he sat down facing the door. Then they gave him a groat, which he put in his pocket, a crust of bread, which he ate, and a full bowle of ale, which he drank off at a draught. After this he got up from the cricket and pronounced, with a composed gesture, the ease and rest of the Soul departed, for which he would pawn his own soul.

In a related procedure, a *watching-candle* or group of *ghost-candles* to ward off ghosts were often burned by a *pernoctalian*, one who sat up all night with a corpse. The candle-watcher's task was eased in the 1600s, when the stimulating effects of tobacco helped him stay awake during these long vigils, eventually known as "tobacco-nights." An ancient forerunner of this custom was used by Butler as an allusion to unrequited love:

> Love in your heart burns
> As fire in antique Roman urns,
> To warm the dead, and vainly light
> Those only that see nothing by 't.

Another term related to the sinne-eater, *fee-grief*, referred to mourning acted out by a substitute hired with *sinne-money*, offerings given to atone for one's wrongdoings. About this time, the Church boldly decreed that only a third of one's estate should be left to relatives, opening the way for vast sums of "guilt money" to be bequeathed to the local parish to ease the departed's pains in purgatory.

RESURRECTIONIST * Formerly known as an "all-night man," a lowly grave robber employed during the eighteenth and nineteenth centuries—for handsome sums of money—to exhume and steal recently buried bodies from their "eternity boxes" in churchyards. The resurrectionists' patrons were usually anatomy schools, their students and surgeons forming "anatomy clubs" for whom cadavers were legally all but unavailable at that time in England. From these gangs of cemetery pilferers, Dickens, in *A Tale of Two Cities*, developed

the character of resurrectionist Jerry Cruncher, who when asked by his son what a "resurrection-man" was, initially pretended ignorance. Upon being pressed about the "goods" they dealt in, he replied,

> "His goods is a branch of scientific goods."
> "Persons' bodies, ain't it, father?"
> "I believe it is something of that sort."

After sensing an interest by his son in this line of work, Cruncher proudly offered some practical advice on becoming a resurrectionist: "Be careful to develop your talents, and never say no more than you can help to nobody, and there's no telling at the present time what you may not come to be fit for."

In 1818, a patent was granted for an iron coffin equipped with a specially flanged lid with spring clips, designed to shut permanently and withstand the onslaught of body snatchers. After originally refusing to allow armored coffins to be buried in their cemeteries, the Church of England lost a lawsuit to relatives of a deceased parishioner and reluctantly agreed. The clergy did, however, charge extra for interring this state-of-the-art coffin since, they reasoned, the coffin and its contents took longer to decompose and would therefore be around longer. Scotland apparently had problems with resurrectionists as well, as Jamieson's *Scottish Dictionary* included the entry *mort-safe:* "A frame of cast iron with which a coffin is surrounded during five or six weeks for the purpose of preventing the robbery of the grave." By the late 1820s, body snatching had become so commonplace, and the public so alarmed, that graveyard "watch houses" were built, and crypts underwent a popular revival. This clandestine practice eventually disappeared due largely to the British Anatomy Act of 1832, which allowed more legal donations. As the supply caught up with demand, only ghoulish material for Gothic novels and horror films remained of the resurrectionist.

ARVAL-SUPPER * Fifteenth-century post-funeral banquet celebrating an inheritance. This name was based on the eleventh-century *arfname*, the "name of an heir," itself a triple composite of Old Norse *arfr*, an inheritance, Welsh *arwhyl*, a eulogy, and Old English *ale*, a feast. The arval-supper was usually given by the primary heir, though occasionally paid for by the deceased, lasting as an institution into the 1800s. This obscure forerunner of modern funeral procedures appears to have been largely focused on the dead man's property, as explained by Hazlitt:

> On the decease of any person possessed of valuable effects, the friends and neighbors of the family are invited to dinner on the day of interment. . . . This custom seems of distant antiquity, and was a solemn festival, made at the time of publically exposing the corps, to exculpate

the heir and those entitled to the possessions of the deceased from fines and mulcts to the Lord of the Manor and from all accusation of having used violence, so that the persons then convoked might avouch that the person died fairly and without suffering any personal injury. The dead were thus exhibited by antient nacions and perhaps the custom was introduced here by the Romans.

Funerals were an important opportunity to display one's station in life, even after death, as is apparent from E. M. Wright's partial inventory of the arval-supper of a farmer who died near Whitby in 1760: "110 dozen penny loaves, 9 large hams, 8 legs of veal, 20 stone of beef [14 pounds to the stone], 16 stone of mutton, 15 stone of Cheshire cheese and 30 ankers of ale."

The more intimate arval-supper of Margaret Atkinson in 1544 required the following arrangements:

> The next Sunday after her burial, there will be provided two dozen [loaves] of bread, a kilderken of ale, two gammons of bacon, three shoulders of mutton and . . . rabbits. Desiring all the parish, as well rich as poor, to take part thereof, and a table to be set in the midst of the church, with every thing necessary thereto.

Part of the record of the fourth Lord of Berkeley's 1368 arval preparations stated:

> Until his interment, the reeve of his manor of Hinton spent three quarters and seaven bushells in beanes in fatting one hundred geese towards his funerall, and divers other reeves of other manors the like, in geese, duckes and other pultry.

According to Roman writer Wormius, it was once prohibited for anyone to pay his respects to the deceased until he had presented an offering of food and drink commensurate with his station: "One thing principally attended to on this occasion was that, in honour of the defunct . . . vast bowls were drunk and his successor bound himself by vow to perform some memorable achievement."

MANQUELLER * A companion word to Shakespeare's "womanqueller" for a murderer and later a town executioner,

dating back at least to the thirteenth century. In many parts of Europe the manqueller was in a social class by himself, as he and his children were not generally allowed to socialize normally with others or have another trade, except for such work as torturer, brothel-keeper, *knacker* (dead animal remover), and possibly butcher. A bizarre punishment for women guilty of adultery required them to dance with the manqueller. Prostitutes, however, were capable of "cheating the hangman," as their acceptance of a condemned man's proposal of marriage sometimes bought his freedom, though her favor was almost always refused. This custom prompted Shakespeare's line from *Twelfth Night*, "Many a good hanging saves a bad marriage." Conversely, with his practical knowledge of anatomy, which gave him a certain mystique, the manqueller was sometimes considered to be akin to a shaman. He was privately approached for special occult preparations and body parts that might insure health or luck in a venture, as we learn from Grose's *Antiquarian Repository:*

> A dead man's hand is supposed to have the quality of dispelling tumours, such as wens or swelled glands, by stroking it nine times, the place effected. It seems as if the hand of a person dying a violent death was deemed particularly efficacious, as it very frequently happens that nurses bring children to be stroked with the hands of executed criminals, even whilst they are still hanging on the gallows.

Hangmen supplemented their incomes in a number of ways, such as selling the hand of an executee, which was soaked in oil and used as a torch by rogues attempting to locate hidden treasure. In 1542, this technique of treasure hunting was taken seriously enough that an English statute made it punishable by "pillory for the first offence and death for the second," though Irish thieves continued to use it at least into the 1830s. In addition, noblemen were once expected to provide the hangman a gratuity for his service, which entitled them to be suspended by a more comfortable silken rope. Until the eighteenth century, manquellers also sold ropes used on celebrities as souvenirs, sometimes cutting the cord into multiple sections for the more popular ones, a practice Brand shed some light upon:

> I remember once to have seen at Newcastle-upon-Tyne, after a person executed had been cut down, men climb up upon the gallows and contend for that part of the rope which remained, and which they wished to preserve for some lucky purpose or other. I have lately made the important discovery that it is reckoned a cure for the headache [bound firmly around the temples].

The manqueller's hanging apparatus, called a *derrick*, was named after an infamous hangman, Godfrey Derrick, who practiced his craft on a large clientele of "gallows-ripe" felons at Tyburn prison. It has been estimated that about 50,000 people were executed there between the years 1196 and 1783, including Derrick himself in 1601. Grose reported a special use for the gallows: "The chips or cuttings of a gibbet or gallows, on which one or more persons have been executed or exposed, if worn next the skin in a bag, will cure the ague [fever] or prevent it."

In the late eighteenth century, Dr. Joseph Guillotin felt strongly that execution should be the same for everyone, regardless of a person's rank, position, or wealth. At that time, the privileged were often beheaded with an ax, while the poor were generally hanged, reflecting a longstanding notion that beheading was more dignified. As a result of Guillotin's efforts, a "philanthropic decapitation machine," as he called it, was created, which performed executions "in a twinkling." He asserted that the convicts would feel only a "cool refreshment," a theory he was never able to prove.

———————

OBSEQUY * Shortened from the Latin *obsequium*, it originally meant an "act of compliance," as well as portions of funerary rites. These solemn ceremonies included eulogies that with rare exceptions spoke only of the accomplishments, positive attributes, and overall benevolence of the deceased. Jamieson attempted to put funeral orations into perspective:

> In our own time, when men speak of the dead, especially if anything is said to their dispraise, it is common to qualify it by some phrase, apparently expressive of sympathy or regard . . . while what is said often directly contradicts the mollifying qualification. . . . The ancient Romans, in speaking of the dead, seem to have been afraid, not of merely causing disquietude to them, but of being themselves troubled with their unwelcome visits.

Obsequies could, in Elizabethan times, refer to mourning rituals engaged in by survivors, as with the king's recommendation to Hamlet that he limit his "obsequious sorrow" for his recently slain father. Shakespeare also demonstrated this term's meaning in a question by Juliet's suitor, Paris, after her death in *Romeo and Juliet:*

> What cursed foot wanders this way to-night,
> To cross my obsequies and true love's rites?

Obsequiousness, especially the verbal variety, was closely allied to the artful use of euphemism, which itself came from Greek and meant "to speak well of." One example of this involved an unpopular and eccentric Madame Cresswell who, according to Hazlitt,

> . . . desired to have a sermon preached at her funeral, for which the preacher was to have ten pounds, but upon this express condition: that he was to say nothing but what was well of her. He, after a sermon preached on the general subject of morality and the good uses to be made of it, concluded with saying, by terms of his agreement, "she was born with the name Cresswell, she lived in Clerkenwell, and she died in Bridewell [prison]."

Agreeable utterances were not the only odd things to be heard at funerals, according to sixteenth-century writer John Veron, who commented upon the "rather unsemely howling that Papists use for the salvation of theyr dead, therby under a pretense of godlinesse, picking the purses of the pore, simple and ignorant people." Grose gave a clue as to why men politely remove their hats at funerals: "If you meet a funeral procession, or one passes by you, always take off your hat; this keeps all the evil spirits attending the body in good humour."

UPAS * Adjective from the eighteenth and nineteenth centuries for "malevolent or deadly power," borrowed from the name of Indonesia's once legendary upas tree, which was believed extremely fatal. The tree's pernicious influence was inferred from natives' use of its milky sap as poison applied to arrow tips, and a "putrid steam" said to emanate from it. One fraudulent account, supposedly by a Dutch physician, reported of this tree: "Not a tree, nor blade of grass . . . not a beast or bird, reptile or living thing lives in the vicinity [of the upas]. . . . 1,600 refugees [were] encamped within 14 miles of it, and all but 300 died within two months." George Steevens, a Shakespearean commentator, was best known for his many fabulous hoaxes, including the preceding story of the upas's potent malignancy. He chose magazines or popular newspapers for the promulgation of clever ruses such as this, and signed them with fictitious names calculated to disarm suspicion. In his *Book of Days*, Chambers profiled Steevens's work:

> The entire life of Steevens has been characterised as displaying an unparalleled series of arch deceptions, tinctured with much malicious ingenuity. . . . It is impossible to calculate the full amount of mischief that may be produced by such means—literature may be disfigured and falsehood take the place of fact.

Steevens's 1783 account of the upas in *London Magazine* was unwittingly applauded by Charles Darwin's grandfather Erasmus, and introduced in the elder's book, *Botanic Garden*. The tree's deadly reputation spread through general literature into the 1840s as an uncontested fact, until artists were called upon to present visual renderings of the tree surrounded by legendary fatalities. To this day, the upas's scientific name—*Antiaris toxicaria*—denotes toxicity.

LIGHTNING-BEFORE-DEATH * Psychological "last gasp" phenomenon from Elizabethan times, usually occurring just before death. It was sometimes accompanied by a "delightfully sweet smell," called the *odour of sanctity*, said in medieval times to occur when angels were present at someone's deathbed, as well as by a long, deep inspiration called a "fetch." Lightning-before-death was described by Nares as

> A proverbial phrase, partly deduced from observation of some extraordinary effort made in sick persons just before death, partly from the superstitious notion of an ominous mirth supposed to come on at that time, without any ostensible reason.

Samuel Pepys wrote in his 1663 diary of the events preceding the queen's "lightning": "It seems she was so ill as to be shaved and pidgeons put to her feet, and to have extreme unction given her by the priests, who were so long about it that the doctors were angry."

In his 1670 collection of proverbs, Ray made a striking analogy: "This is generally observed of sick persons, that a little before they die, their pains leave them, and their understanding and memory return, as a candle just before it goes out gives a great blaze." Seventeenth-century poet Edmund Gayton commented upon this profound occurrence:

> Not that I lightning or thunder feare,
> Unless that lightning before death appear.

In *Romeo and Juliet*, after slaying Paris, Romeo asks himself,

> How oft' when men are at the point of death
> Have they been merry? which their keepers call
> A lightning before death.

225

Although the name has long been forgotten, the dramatic outward manifestation of this emotional experience survived into the twentieth century as sometimes seen in death scenes from vintage cinema.

TWYCHILD * An elderly man or woman, undoubtedly inspired by Shakespeare's description of the "seven ages" of man from *As You Like It*. After reflecting upon old age, the bard concluded:

> Last scene of all,
> That ends this strange eventful history,
> Is second childishness, and mere oblivion,
> Sans teeth, sans eyes, sans taste, sans everything.

Twychild meant literally "twice a child," from *twy*, "twice," and was pronounced "twichel" for verbal economy. John Davies wrote of this stage of life considered to herald the beginning of the end, in his 1612 *Muse's Sacrifice:* "Man growne twy-childe is at door of death." Later in the seventeenth century, English poet John Milton, inspired by Shakespeare's comments regarding age, concluded in his masterpiece *Paradise Regained*, "The child is father of the man."

SAUNCE-BELL * The *soulbell* or *passing-bell*, which was believed intolerable to evil spirits. Saunce-bells were commonly rung since the eighth century to keep these malicious spirits away from the souls of the nearly or soon-to-be deceased as they made their way from this life to the next. Grose's *Antiquarian Repository* stated that it

> . . . was anciently rung for two purposes: one, to bespeak the prayers of all good Christians for a soul just depart-

ing; the other, to drive away the evil spirits who stood at the bed's foot and about the house, ready to seize their prey, or at least to molest and terrify the soul in its passage. By the ringing of the bell they were kept aloof, and the soul, like a hunted hare, gained the start, or had what sportsmen call the "law."

Robert Herrick's poem *The Spell* alluded to this belief:

Give the tapers here their light,
Ring the Saints-Bell, to affright
Far from hence the evill Sp'rite.

A sixteenth-century English ordinance recommended:

When anye Christian bodie is in passing, that the bell be tolled and that the curate be speciallie called for to comforte the sicke person; and after the time of his passinge to ringe no more, but one shorte peale . . . before the buriall and another peale after the buriall.

The term *bell-penny* represented the money set aside for the ringing of one's passing-bell and funeral expenses, such as the cost of the seventeenth-century custom called a *shoulder-feast*, a dinner for the pall-bearers after a funeral. Harland explained the Church's rationale for charging a higher fee for the ringing of their largest bells:

Hence the high charge for tolling the great bell of the church, which, being louder, the evil spirits must go further off to be clear of its sound; besides, being heard further off, it would likewise procure the dying man a greater number of prayers.

Until 1830, in Catholic churches, the interment ended with a flourish: ". . . a merry peal of the bells . . . [as] doubtless the greater the clang of the bells, the further the flight of the fiends waiting to seize the soul of the departed." Besides protecting the recently departed, saunce-bells were thought capable of pro-

viding protection from storms and pestilence. The following seventeenth-century monk's doggerel, translated from Latin, gave a few additional uses for the penetrating tintinnabulation of medieval bells:

Men's deaths I tell, by doleful knell;
Lightning and thunder, I break asunder;
On Sabbath all, To church I call;
The sleepy head, I raise from bed;
The winds so fierce, I do disperse;
Men's cruel rage, I do assuage.

Bibliography

Amt, Emelie. *Women's Lives in Medieval Europe*. New York: Routledge, 1993.

Ashton, John. *Social Life in the Reign of Queen Anne*. New York: Scribner and Welford, 1883.

Atwater, Donald. *Penguin Dictionary of Saints*. Baltimore: Penguin, 1965.

Bailey, Nathaniel. *An Universal Etymological Dictionary*. London, 1749.

Baring-Gould, Sabine. *The Book of Werewolves*. London: Smith, Elder, 1865.

Barrister, A. *Every Man's Own Lawyer*. London: Lockwood, 1863.

Blount, Thomas. *Glossographia*. 1656. Reprint. Hildesheim: Georg Olms, 1972.

Boorstin, Daniel. *The Discoverers*. New York: Random House, 1983.

Brand, John. *Observations on Popular Antiquities*. London, 1813.

Brewer, Ebenezer C. *Brewer's Dictionary of Phrase and Fable*. New York: Harper & Row, 1970.

Briggs, Asa. *A Social History of England*. London: Penguin, 1983.

Buck, Charles, Rev. *Theological Dictionary*. Philadelphia: J. J. Woodward, 1835.

Burne, Charlotte S. *The Handbook of Folklore*. London: Sidgewick & Jackson, 1883.

Butler, Samuel. *Hudibras*. 1663. Reprint. London: Henry Bohn, 1859.

Chambers, Robert. *The Book of Days*. London: W. & R. Chambers, 1864.

Chaucer, Geoffrey. *The Canterbury Tales*. London: Oxford University Press, 1947.

Cotgrave, Randle. *A Dictionary of the French and English Tongues*. 1611.

Craig, W. J. *Shakespeare: The Complete Works*. Oxford: Oxford University Press, 1974.

Davies, T. Lewis. *Supplemental Glossary*. London: George Bell, 1881.

Dorson, Richard. *The British Folklorists: A History*. Chicago: University of Chicago Press, 1968.

Dunglison, Robley, M.D. *A Dictionary of Medical Science*. Philadelphia: Lea & Blanchard, 1844.

Dyche, Thomas, and William Pardon. *A New General English Dictionary*. 1740. Reprint. Hildesheim: Georg Olms, 1972.

Erickson, Carolly. *Great Harry: The Extravagant Life of Henry VIII*. New York: Summit Books, 1980.

Foote, Thomas, Dr. *Plain Home Talk About the Human System*. 1898.

Franklin, Benjamin. *Poor Richard: The Almanacks*. New York: Heritage Press, 1964.

Gerarde, John. *The Herball, or General Historie of Plants*. 1597. Reprint. New York: Dover, 1975.

Gies, Frances, and Joseph Gies. *Life in a Medieval Village*. New York: Harper & Row, 1990.

Green, Jonathon. *Chasing the Sun: Dictionary Makers and the Dictionaries They Made*. New York: Henry Holt, 1996.

Gregor, Walter. *Notes on the Folklore of North-East Scotland*, 1881.

Grose, Francis. *Provincial Glossary*. London: Edward Jeffery, 1811.

―――. *A Classical Dictionary of the Vulgar Tongue*. Reprint. New York: Barnes & Noble, 1963.

Hall, John. *Select Observations on English Bodies*. 1657. Reprint. Privately published, 1993.

Halliwell, James. *A Dictionary of Archaic and Provincial Words*. 1855. Reprint. New York: AMS Press, 1973.

Hammond, Peter. *Food and Feast in Medieval England*. Phoenix Mill, Far Thrupp, Stroud, Gloucestershire: Alan Sutton, 1993.

Harland, John. *Lancashire Folk-lore*. London: Frederick Warne, 1867.

Hazlitt, W. C. *Dictionary of Faiths and Folklore*. London: Reeves & Turner, 1905.

Henderson, William. *Notes on the Northern Counties of England and the Borders*, 1866.

Herrick, Robert. *The Poetical Works*. London: Oxford University Press, 1921.

Hole, Christina. *The Encyclopedia of Superstitions*. Oxford: Helicon, 1980.

———. *A Dictionary of British Folk Customs*. Oxford: Helicon, 1995.

Hone, William. *The Everyday Book*. London: Hunt & Clark, 1826.

Hunter, Robert. *The Encyclopedic Dictionary*. Philadelphia: Syndicate, 1894.

Jamieson, John. *An Etymological Dictionary of the Scottish Language*. 4 vols. Paisley: Alexander Gardner, 1808.

Jerrold, Douglas. *Mrs. Caudle's Curtain Lectures*. New York: Appleton, 1866.

Johnson, Samuel. *A New Dictionary of the English Language*. London: George Virtue, 1843.

Judges, A. V. *The Elizabethan Underworld*, 1930.

Knowlson, T. Sharper. *The Origins of Popular Superstitions*. London: T. Werner Laurie, 1930.

Langland, William. *Piers Plowman*. c. 1377. Reprint. Oxford: Oxford University Press, 1992.

Latham, Robert, and William Matthews, eds. *The Diary of Samuel Pepys*. Berkeley: University of California Press, 1970–1983.

Leslie, Robert C. *Old Sea Wings, Ways and Words*. London: Chapman & Hall, 1890.

McCall, Andrew. *The Medieval Underworld*. New York: Barnes & Noble, 1979.

Mackay, Charles. *Extraordinary Popular Delusions and the Madness of Crowds*. New York: Farrar, Straus & Giroux, 1932.

———. *Lost Beauties of the English Language*. Reprint. London: Bibliophile Books, 1987.

Malkin, Benjamin. *The Scenery, Antiquities and Biography of South Wales*, 1804.

Mayhew, Henry. *London Labour and the London Poor*. 1861. Reprint. New York: Dover, 1968.

Melville, Herman. *Moby Dick or, The Whale*. Norwalk: Easton Press, 1977.

Nares, Robert. *A Glossary [of] Phrases, Names and Allusions to Customs & Proverbs*. John Russel Smith, 1859.

Ogilvie, John. *The Comprehensive English Dictionary*. London: Blackie & Son, 1865.

Opie, Iona. *Oxford Dictionary of Nursery Rhymes*. Oxford: Oxford University Press, 1985.

Partridge, Eric. *A Dictionary of Slang and Unconventional English*. New York: Macmillan, 1956.

Read, Carveath. *Man and His Superstitions*. London: Cambridge University Press, 1925.

Ridley, Jasper. *The Tudor Age*. New York: Overlook Press, 1990.

Scot, Reginald. *The Discoverie of Witchcraft*. 1584. Reprint. New York: Dover, 1989.

Shipley, Joseph. *Dictionary of Early English*. New York: New York Philosophical Library, 1955.

Simpson, J. A. *The Concise Oxford Dictionary of Proverbs*. Oxford: Oxford University Press, 1982.

Simpson, J. A., and E.S.C. Weiner, eds. *The Oxford English Dictionary, Second Edition, on Compact Disc*. New York: Oxford University Press, 1992.

Sisam, Celia. *The Oxford Book of Medieval English Verse*. Oxford: Clarendon Press, 1973.

Skeat, Walter. *A Glossary of Tudor and Stuart Words*. Oxford: Clarendon Press, 1914.

—————. *An Etymological Dictionary of the English Language*. Oxford: Oxford University Press, 1974.

Smith, Eliza. *The Compleat Housewife*. 1758. Reprint. London: Studio Editions, 1994.

Smollett, Tobias. *Roderick Ransom*. 1748. Reprint. London: Dutton, 1967.

Smyth, William Henry. *The Sailor's Word-book: An Alphabetical Digest of Nautical Terms*, 1867.

Stratmann, Francis. *A Middle English Dictionary*. Oxford: Clarendon Press, 1891.

Strutt, Joseph A. *A Compleat View of the . . . People of England*, 1775.

Thompson, C.J.S. *The Hand of Destiny*. London: Rider, 1932.

Timbs, John. *Curiosities of London*. London: David Bogue, 1855.

Topsell, Edward. *The Historie of Foure-Footed Beastes*. 1607. Reprint. New York: Da Capo/Plenum, 1967.

Trevelan, G. M. *Illustrated English Social History*. London: Longman, Green, 1976.

Tristram, W. Outram. *Coaching Days and Coaching Ways*. London: Macmillan, 1888.

Tusser, Thomas. *Five Hundred Points of Good Husbandry*. London: Trubner, 1878.

Visser, Margaret. *The Rituals of Dinner*. New York: Penguin Books, 1992.

Walker, John. *A Critical Pronouncing Dictionary*. Edinburgh: Brown & Nelson, 1835.

Wentworth, Harold. *American Dialect Dictionary*. New York: Thomas Y. Crowell, 1944.

Whitney, William. *The Century Dictionary: An Encyclopedic Lexicon*. New York: Century, 1889.

Williamson, George. *Curious Survivals*. London: Herbert Jenkins, 1923.

Wright, Elizabeth M. *Rustic Speech and Folk-lore*. London: Oxford University Press, 1914.

Wright, Thomas. *Dictionary of Obsolete and Provincial English*. London: Henry Bohn, 1857.

————. *A History of Domestic Manners and Sentiments*. London: Chapman & Hall, 1862.

Index